TWAYNE'S WORLD AUTHORS SERIES

A Survey of the World's Literature

Sylvia E. Bowman, Indiana University

GENERAL EDITOR

SWEDEN

Leif Sjöberg
State University of New York at Stony Brook

EDITOR

Carl Jonas Love Almqvist

TWAS 401

Carl Jonas Love Almqvist

CARL JONAS LOVE ALMQVIST

By BERTIL ROMBERG

University of Lund

Translated from the Swedish by
STEN LIDÉN

TWAYNE PUBLISHERS
A DIVISION OF G. K. HALL & CO., BOSTON

Library of Congress Cataloging in Publication Data

Romberg, Bertil.
 Carl Jonas Love Almqvist.

 (Twayne's world authors series ; TWAS 401)
 Bibliography: pp. 189–97
 Includes index.
 1. Almqvist, Carl Jonas Love, 1793–1866.
I. Title.
PT9729.Z5R6   839.7'8'609   76–16859
ISBN 0–8057–6241–8

MANUFACTURED IN THE UNITED STATES OF AMERICA

Contents

About the Author

Bertil Romberg was born in 1925 in Helsingborg, Sweden. He graduated from the University of Lund with the thesis *Studies in the narrative technique of the first-person novel* (1962), and has since then been docent (assistant professor) in Literary history at the same university. In 1970 he published a book on how to analyze novels, *Att läsa epik*, and in 1968 he edited Almqvist's letters. He has published studies and articles on narrative technique, on Strindberg and on Almqvist. Since 1968 he is a member of the editorial committee of *Orbis Litterarum*.

Preface

The life and works of nineteenth-century Swedish author Carl Jonas Love Almqvist are still read and discussed widely in his native country. His brilliance and scope are of great dimension, and his opinions and ideas strike us as surprisingly modern. All this ought to earn him a place of honor at the international Parnassus, but unfortunately the indifference of much of the world to the Swedish language—which he handled with such mastery—has precluded this possibility.

I have illustrated the following discussion of Almqvist with ample quotations from his writing, especially his journalism and letters.

My friends Sten Lidén and Harold H. Borland have spared no effort in the search to find the right English word, the Swedish Institute has contributed with a generous grant, and Ingrid, my wife, has stood by me from the first outline to the last proofs. My hearty thanks to all of them.

BERTIL ROMBERG

University of Lund

Chronology

1793 November 28: Carl Jonas Love Almqvist born in Stockholm, son of Army Paymaster Carl Gustaf Almqvist and Birgitta Lovisa Gjörwell.

1806 August 8: Birgitta Lovisa Gjörwell dies.

1808 June 11: Almqvist matriculated at Uppsala University.

1814– Tutor to the Hisinger family in Stockholm. The summers
1820 of 1814–17 spent at the Hisinger estate in the south of Finland.

1815 Almqvist conferred the degree of Master of Arts.

1815– Official at the Ministry of Education (assistant chancery
1823 clerk, November 25, 1815; copying clerk, December 6, 1817; registrar, February 13, 1822; resignation, August 27, 1823).

1816 Almqvist elected member of the patriotic society, Manhemsförbundet.

1817 January: Elected member of the Swedenborg society, Pro Fide et Caritate. November: Helps to found the society Manna-Samfund.

1822 *Amorina* printed and destroyed.

1824 January 15: Almqvist leaves Stockholm to settle down with some like-minded friends as crofters in Värmland, where he stayed a year and a half. March 4: Marries Anna Maria Lundström (1797–1868), a brewer's daughter from Uppland.

1825 The Almqvists' son Ludvig (1825–86) is born. Almqvist returns to Stockholm for good.

1826 October: teacher at the Swedish Academy of Military Sciences of Karlberg (until April 28, 1828).

1828 January 2: teacher at Nya elementarskolan in Stockholm. Headmaster of this school, November 16, 1829–September 14, 1841.

1829 The Almqvists' daughter Maria Lovisa (1829–93) is born.

1833 The first parts of *Törnrosens bok* (*The Book of the Wild Rose*) published.
1837 June 11: Almqvist ordained at Uppsala.
1838 Almqvist unsuccessfully applies for the Chair of Aesthetics and Modern Languages at the University of Lund.
1839 Almqvist begins to contribute to the liberal newspaper, *Aftonbladet*, in October he signs a contract with Hierta to become a permanent contributor. In December he publishes *Det går an* (*Sara Videbeck*).
1840– April 1, 1840: On leave from Nya elementarskolan. Cau-
1841 tioned by the Cathedral Chapter of Uppsala on account of *Sara Videbeck* and *Marjam*. August 1840–February 1841: Studying in Paris and London. September 14: dismissal from Nya elementarskolan.
1844 Almqvist also begins to contribute to *Jönköpingsbladet*.
1845– November 1845–March 1846: journey to Germany and
1846 Denmark. April 1, 1846: Employed by *Aftonbladet* as a permanent staff member. October 27: Appointed regimental chaplain of the Royal Life Guards.
1851 June: Charged with forging and stealing promissory notes and attempting to murder by poisoning. Leaves the country. August 22: Arrives in New York. Stays fourteen years in America.
1853 The Court-Martial of Appeal in Stockholm passes judgment.
1854 Almqvist is removed from his post as regimental chaplain. June 11: Marries Emma Nugent (1786–1867) in Philadelphia.
1865 July 17: Leaves America. Arrives at Bremen in October.
1866 September 26: Almqvist dies in Bremen.
1901 Almqvist's mortal remains transferred to Solna Cemetery, outside of Stockholm.

CHAPTER 1

Life and Times

I Origin and Early Life

CARL Jonas Love Almqvist was born in Stockholm on November 28, 1793, the son of Army Paymaster Carl Gustaf Almqvist (1768–1846) and Birgitta Lovisa (Brite Louise) Gjörwell (1768–1806).

On his father's side, Almqvist was descended from clergymen and peasants. His paternal grandfather was a professor of theology and a dean, and an uncle was Bishop of Härnösand. In the middle of the 1790s his father changed his profession and took up farming, and Almqvist's childhood was spent in the heart of Uppland on the estates of Sätra and Antuna.

On his mother's side, Almqvist was descended through his maternal grandfather from the middle-class Stockholm family of Feif, well known in the seventeenth and eighteenth centuries and originating from Scotland. His maternal grandfather was the pious and learned publicist, Carl Christoffer Gjörwell (1731–1811), who was to play an important role in the upbringing of his grandson. The poet's mother was a fragile and romantic person who died when her son was only thirteen.

Among Almqvist's forefathers we find representatives of all the four estates, and—in the various social surroundings—learned, practical, romantic, and restless personalities. Almqvist mentions his parents several times in his letters, but I prefer to quote his friend Lars Johan Hierta, who tells us how the poet used to group his hereditary dispositions:

He also used to say, at least he sometimes said to us, that in him there seemed to be two souls: a paymaster's soul that he had inherited from his father, and a poetic soul, a heritage from his mother, with a deep feeling for the beauty of nature, poetry, and music; that his

11

disposition and manner at any given moment depended on which of these souls was prevailing and that they were often in a kind of conflict with each other.[1]

But let us leave Almqvist's heritage and turn to his milieu and his time. When Almqvist was born the Kingdom of Sweden was a large country with a small population.[2] It was a markedly agrarian country: at the start of the new century three-fourths of its inhabitants lived by agriculture. Iron was still the most important export commodity, and half of it went to England. The towns were small and fairly insignificant; at the turn of the century Stockholm, the capital, had about 70,000 inhabitants. Academic education was available in Sweden at the two universities of Uppsala and Lund; in Åbo in Finland there was a third university.

In the last decades of the eighteenth century, under Gustav III, there had developed a culture and literature that are usually designated as Gustavian. Carl Michael Bellman and Johan Henrik Kellgren, the leading poets, had died in the 1790s, but the Gustavian school, with its roots in Enlightenment and French culture, was still predominant at the beginning of the new century. In the first decade of the nineteenth century reports of European, particularly German, Romanticism reached Swedish literary circles. In the 1810s a Romantic school of poetry came forth in Sweden represented by Atterbom, Geijer, Stagnelius, and Tegnér, who were to make the 1820s a golden age of Swedish literature. Almqvist joined this group to begin with.

Almqvist was well prepared to cope with the ideas of his time. His education was scrupulous and extensive; it bore the stamp of old Gjörwell's comprehensive erudition. In 1808, not yet fifteen, Almqvist matriculated at Uppsala University where he focused his studies on philosophy and history. In 1815 he defended a thesis, *Monumentorum veterum Historiæ Sveogothicæ Prolegomena*, was awarded the degree of Master of Arts, and left Uppsala.

Almqvist's studies in Uppsala were energetic and comprehensive; he developed a thorough knowledge of philosophy, modern as well as ancient. He also got acquainted with the new German Romantic philosophy and literature. In an interview many years later, Almqvist declared that he had studied "all the philosophers, from Plato and Aristotle to Spinoza, Schelling, and Böhme." On the same occasion he also stated that it was at Uppsala that he made the acquaintance of Swedenborg, whose writings he studied closely. As far as his contemporary fellow-students in Uppsala were concerned, he was at first "friends with the Phosphorists, but his bent for mathematics separated him from them."[3]

If Almqvist's studies were intense, his encounters with other students were accordingly limited. In fact, two of the leaders of Swedish Romanticism, Atterbom and Palmblad, studied at Uppsala at the same time as Almqvist, and it was there that they published the literary journal *Phosphoros*, which became the journal of Swedish Romanticism as *Athenäum* had been that of German Romanticism. (*Phosphoros* was also to give the name of "Phosphorists" to the active group of Uppsala Romantics.) That Almqvist had studied the printed manifestos of the Phosphorists is well known, but he made neither Atterbom's nor Palmblad's personal acquaintance until about 1820 though all three of them had taken their degree in 1815.

Not yet twenty-two, with his Master of Arts diploma in his pocket, Almqvist approached the Civil Service Department in Stockholm and, in November 1815, was appointed assistant chancery clerk at the Department of Ecclesiastical Affairs (i.e., the Ministry of Education). Incidentally, he was here the colleague of Erik Johan Stagnelius, one of the greatest lyric poets of Swedish Romanticism. But Stagnelius was a hermit, and the relationship between them was never intimate. Stagnelius, who was also born in 1793, died in 1823 when Almqvist was still on the threshold of his literary career.

During the eight years that Almqvist discharged his not very heavy duties he showed an increasing dislike for his life as a civil servant. A letter he wrote at the beginning of 1823 to his uncle, Bishop Almqvist, reveals the poet's disgust, verging on desperation, at the monotony of the work and the striking injustice institutionalized in the civil service.

There is something of a *Sturm und Drang* note in the desperation of the nearly thirty-year-old poet at not being allowed to follow his vocation. Almqvist's civil service term was actually drawing to an end. Threatened with legal proceedings for neglect of duty, he was forced to resign in August 1823. His letters reveal a great deal about his view of the civil service. However, Almqvist portrayed the very essence of bureaucracy most lucidly—and crushingly—in the brilliant satirical myth, *"Ormus och Ariman"* ("Ormus and Ariman").

He was engaged in a number of activities in addition to his civil service work. From 1814 to 1820 he was employed by the wealthy cavalry captain, Hisinger, to tutor his son Fridolf. In winter Almqvist lived with the Hisinger family in Stockholm and in summer at Hisinger's estate Fagervik in the south of Finland. He seems to have taken his task as a tutor very seriously and to have undertaken it with zeal. In the Hisinger family, Almqvist came to know a milieu accented by Gustavian culture, with liberal ideas derived from the Enlightenment, all of which might have formed an agreeable contrast to the civil service atmosphere.

In 1816, after his scholarly studies, Almqvist published the small tract *Vad är kärlek?* (*What is Love?*). The title raises a question which, in various forms, was to interest Almqvist enormously throughout his life. It must be pointed out, however, that in this first publication Almqvist's opinions are on the whole conservative.

His religious and philosophic studies were continued during his civil service years. In his adolescence he had been strongly influenced by the Moravian sect (through Gjörwell, among others) and, after a crisis in 1813, also by Swedenborgianism. In 1816 he joined Manhemsförbundet, a society with a Gothic-Christian pedagogic program. In 1817 he founded a branch of Manhemsförbundet: Manna-Samfund—of a more exclusive character. Among the romantic and gifted members of these societies were the future General J. A. Hazelius and his brothers, Jonas Wærn, later Cabinet Minister, and the theologians, Henrik Öfverberg and Anders Berg. Sporadically, during different periods, such men of letters as Arvid Afzelius, P. D. Atterbom, C. F. Dahlgren and Anders Fryxell participated. In these societies Almqvist very soon reached a prominent position, and his adepts formed a faithful group of listeners. One over-excited member, Gustaf Hazelius, called Almqvist "the holy man of

God—our prophet—the man sent to cast light on our ideas—he, God's wonderful instrument, held out his beloved hands to us, and we reached the much longed-for land" (*Letters*, p. 7).

Almqvist's letters to the Manhem members are to a large extent religious tracts, both general and private, with philosophic-religious, sometimes hermetic comments. But even if the theories Almqvist propounds may be obscure, he presents them in clearly outlined and explanatory arguments so that these letters resemble short compositions or essays.

In 1820 Almqvist published a volume entitled *Handlingar till upplysning i Manhemsförbundets historia* (*Informative Documents Regarding the History of Manhemsförbundet*), an account of the various ranks within the society and their symbolism and mystic implication. The intent of this ambitious program, which aims toward religious regeneration, is a national culture and an idealization of the life of the farmer.

The success Almqvist had expected did not materialize in spite of the enthusiasm of the young Romanticists.

At that time Almqvist was working on *Amorina*, a large-scale dramatic novel which was highly critical of society, and at the same time stylistically bold and effective in form. It went to press in 1822, but within a few pages of completion, the printing was stopped and the whole edition destroyed. Almqvist's uncle, the Bishop of Härnösand, is believed to have intervened, anxious to save his nephew's career. It was 1839 before *Amorina* was eventually published and this time in thoroughly revised form. We may say that Almqvist was stopped on the threshold of his literary career; not until eleven years later did he publish another work of fiction, "*Jaktslottet*" ("The Hunting Seat"), the first piece in *The Book of the Wild Rose*.

These years between *Amorina* and "The Hunting Seat" also witness Almqvist's various anxiety-stricken efforts to enter upon a new career in society. The suppression of *Amorina* was evidently of great psychologic importance to him. It must have seemed like a defeat, accenting his inability to get on in the civil service (which in turn was probably due to his general dissatisfaction with life). It was a kind of vicious circle. Everything now appeared to enhance the appeal of his Rousseauesque dream of living the peasant's idyllic and idealized life, close to

the earth and far away from an unnatural urban culture. Unlike
other enthusiasts with similar not very original dreams, however,
Almqvist put his theories into practice. For a year and a half—
from January 1824 until the summer of 1825—he lived as a
farmer in Värmland in a small community of individuals who
shared his interest in an alternative way of life.

II *Marriage and Farming in Värmland;*
Writing and Teaching in Stockholm

In Värmland, Almqvist divided his energies between writing
and farming. (When writing, he liked to call himself "Love
Carlsson, yeoman farmer.") He married, and life seemed pleasant at first. But the "Love Carlsson" experiment was not an
unqualified success. Several of his friendships ended, and others
cooled. More fatal, however, was his marriage to Anna Maria
Lundström, a simple peasant girl who had previously worked
as nursemaid to Almqvist's younger brothers and sisters. In
spite of good intentions, the marriage was unhappy, and after
the return to Stockholm, he became more and more convinced
that his wife, with her slow, morose nature, was inadequate for
him. And this state of affairs persisted for the rest of their married life. His marriage appeared to him to be at its best when
he was away on his innumerable journeys. His letters to his
wife are affectionate and strikingly considerate. To his children,
Ludvig and Marie Louise, he seems to have been the most
loving of fathers.

On the credit side of his farming experiment, however, we
must report that his Värmland years were to all appearances
extremely productive. By all indications it was in Värmland that
Almqvist initiated his *Jordens blomma* (*Flower of the Earth*)
project, intended as a poetic survey of the history of humanity
from the Creation, a gigantic undertaking that, in modified
form, was eventually to emerge as *Törnrosens bok* (*The Book
of the Wild Rose*).

Almqvist's baggage was crammed with manuscripts when he
returned to Stockholm in August 1825. After his failure as both
civil servant and farmer, he went through a difficult period
during which he was reduced to temporary income sources

for his subsistence until 1828, when in earnest he entered into a new career—that of teaching. In this year he was engaged by Nya elementarskolan, Stockholm's famous experimental school, and here he served as principal from 1829 to 1841. At the same time he was commissioned to write textbooks on the most diverse subjects. Thus in 1829 he brought out *Svensk rättstavningslära* (*Swedish Orthography*; twentieth edition 1881) and in 1832 *Svensk språklära* (*A Swedish Grammar*; fourth edition 1854). This category of Almqvist's writings includes manuals of linear drawing, geometry, and arithmetic, a Greek grammar, and a practical textbook of French. The range of his schoolbook writing was indicative of the author's comprehensive knowledge and confident, if not always quite successful, enterprise.

Almqvist continued his philosophic and religious studies and writing, and we know that he often met Swedenborgians and Moravian brothers for theological and philosophical debates.

But while leaning toward the mystical and esoteric, he also needed contact with reality and gratified this desire by means of long journeys. In fact, Almqvist was an assiduous and enthusiastic traveler, and as the years went by, he came to know many parts of Sweden, later Europe, and eventually America. Periodic traveling seems to have been a vital necessity for Almqvist. Leading the free, irresponsible life of a traveler, he relaxed from oppressive worries. But traveling was not primarily an escape from the unpleasantries of everyday life. Traveling also meant searching for something new, new people and new surroundings. The scope of Almqvist's interests made it possible for him to feel at home everywhere, and the frequent changes involved in traveling heightened its stimulus.

During the early 1830s Almqvist fulfilled his teaching duties and also prepared to return to creative writing which he did in 1833 with the first series of *The Book of the Wild Rose*.

Then a tragic event occurred which was to shock many in Almqvist's circle of acquaintances and friends. In June 1833 Almqvist's servant and foster-daughter, Stina Holfelt, and his friend, Gustaf Hazelius, committed suicide by drowning themselves together in Edsviken, near Stockholm. Their deaths were believed to be related to their adherence to the view of death promulgated by Almqvist both verbally and in writing. Rumors developed, and many of Almqvist's contemporaries—probably unjustly—found his role in the affair nebulous. The tragedy was given a lasting memorial in one of Almqvist's most beautiful *songes*, "*Den drunknade simmerskan*" ("The Drowned Swimmer").

However, the reactions to the suicide of the couple indicate that the view of Almqvist held by his contemporaries began to be dominated by his more mysterious, elusive, and unexpected traits.

In the same year, 1833, the first installments of Almqvist's *Book of the Wild Rose* appeared, and the floodgates opened. All the manuscripts he had stored in the years following his failure with *Amorina* were now revised, finished, and printed in quick succession together with new works, and consequently, in the 1830s Almqvist was regarded as incredibly productive, a veritable wizard of letters.

The long interval between the writing and publication of many of his works has raised a number of intricate chronological problems. This is especially true of his unique musical poems, "*Songes*," which were not published until 1849 though they had for the most part been written in the 1820s or 1830s.

Some bibliographical information about *The Book of the Wild Rose* is necessary at this point. Almqvist's principal work, it was published between 1833 and 1851 in seventeen parts and two series: the first, the duodecimo edition, consisting of fourteen small-sized volumes from the years 1833 to 1851, and the second, the imperial octavo edition, consisting of three magnificent closely printed volumes from 1839 to 1850. The long tale, "The Hunting Seat," provides the framework for this vast and imposing collection of novels, short stories, lyrics, drama, music, essays, and tracts. The principal characters and narrators are the old nobleman, Hugo Löwenstjerna, and the farmer, Richard Furumo.

The first *Wild Rose* volumes were well received, and in 1834, the brilliant novel, *Drottningens juvelsmycke* (*The Queen's Jewel*), was published. Suddenly, mid-decade, Almqvist's work was proving him to be one of the great writers of his time.

At first Almqvist was successful as principal of Nya elementarskolan. The teaching ideas that were tried there—for example, free activity among the pupils—were largely his invention and

turned out to have long lasting merit. Former pupils confirm—
and his education writings indicate—that Almqvist was a born
teacher. Nevertheless, it is evident that by about midway
through the decade, he became dissatisfied with his humdrum
existence. He now began to look feverishly for a new career
and new livelihood. He was ordained in 1837, and in 1838 he
applied for a professorship of aesthetics and modern languages
in Lund. His ordination, however, did not lead to an ecclesiastical
post any higher than the office of regimental chaplain to the
Royal Life Guards, and this not until 1846. The professorship
went to K. A. Hagberg, the well known translator of Shakespeare.

A remarkable letter to Hazelius dated July 7, 1837, fore-
shadows Almqvist's future development in many respects; he
now feels compelled to rouse, to shock, to offer incentives
against apathy and reaction: "I see distinctly that this must
be the role assigned to me by God." He continues: "Suppose it
should be my responsibility to be a stumbling block? a flaring
fire, in people's stoves?" (*Letters*, p. 113).

This idea was to strike root more deeply in him during the
critical years to follow. To Hazelius he explained his ordination
by saying that he wished to speak to the people; however, it
was not the church that became his forum: it was the
Liberal press.

III *Confrontations with Reality: Poetry and Politics*

Between 1835 and 1838 Almqvist's outlook on life changed
completely. He began to take a keen interest in the real world
around him, in political and social questions. In many respects
he was approaching a new public, his attitude had grown more
popular, and his artistic views more realistic. By 1838 he had
finished two works of particularly sharp social criticism: namely,
the novel, *Sara Videbeck*, and the political pamphlet, *Europeiska
missnöjets grunder* (*The Causes of European Discontent*). They
were in the print or in proof stage when, at the last moment,
Almqvist stopped the publication of these controversial books.

The four volumes of *The Book of the Wild Rose* that were
published in December 1838 show Almqvist at the summit of
his literary powers. Among them are the charming epistolary

story, "*Araminta May*," and the brilliant detective story, "*Palatset*" ("The Palace"). There are also "*Kapellet*" ("The Chapel"), a story which gives a sunny description of the breezy, barren archipelago and which has become one of Almqvist's most popular works, and "*Skällnora kvarn*" ("Skällnora Mill"), a rustic crime story with some of the traits of a Gothic novel.

Among the *Wild Rose* components of 1838 we also find the essay "*Svenska fattigdomens betydelse*" ("The Significance of Swedish Poverty") with the famous analysis of Swedish character. From the world of flowers Almqvist takes his most beautiful symbol of all that is Swedish: the briar rose, the Nordic wild rose, "the picture of poverty, wild grace, and chastity. It represents the whole of our Nordic landscape, concentrated in a phantom" (*CW*, VIII, p. 334). Almqvist contrasts the southern briar rose, juicy, deep red, suggestive of passion with "the small, simple, pink Nordic wild rose with its fine, faint fragrance, the noblest, however, that the air carries." This image, better than any literary explanation, illustrates Almqvist's transition from rich-hued Romantic exoticism through poetic but unadorned national realism onto the poetry of facts.

That longing to write for the people that he manifested in the introduction to "The Significance of Swedish Poverty" takes concrete form in the short series of popular books that Almqvist published in 1839 and 1840. Among the most popular of these were *Grimstahamns nybygge* (*Grimstahamn's New Settlement*) and *Ladugårdsarrendet* (*The Farm Lease*); the former is generally regarded as one of Almqvist's greatest successes.

On the threshold of his new phase, Almqvist attempted something he had tried several times before in his literary career: a theoretical analysis of the essence of art. In 1839 he introduced a series of articles called "*Om poesi i sak*" ("On the Poetry of Facts"; later reprinted in *Monografi* [*Monography*]). In these pieces the romantic poet argues for reality in art and for grappling with problems of the day.

In December 1839, Almqvist's concern with contemporary questions appeared especially pronounced in several tracts and speeches on political, social, and economic issues. Non-fictional prose dominated here as it did nowhere else in the earlier *Wild*

Rose books. A typical title is *"Poesi och politik"* ("Poetry and Politics").

At the same time Almqvist began to publish a new edition, or, more precisely, a new series of *The Book of the Wild Rose,* known as the imperial octavo edition, the first volume of which was also brought out in December 1839. The signals from "On the Poetry of Facts" are less discernible in this edition. In the theological drama, *Marjam,* with motifs from primitive Christian times, Almqvist attacked St. Paul, attracting the deep displeasure of the Cathedral Chapter of Uppsala which, because (since his ordination in 1837) he was one of the clergy of the archdiocese, he would later have cause to regret.

This creative period also produced the previously mentioned book, *Sara Videbeck.*

This novel, which many regard as Almqvist's masterpiece and which was to have such dire consequences for the author, was probably written in the summer of 1838. It came out in December 1839, and a new edition was incorporated in the third volume of the imperial octavo series in 1850.

The plot of *Sara Videbeck* is simple and artless. On a boat trip a young man and a young woman meet. They fall in love with each other and decide to live together in the future though—on her advice—in a free alliance where no formal marriage ceremony will chain them together forever.

It is clear that the work was intended as a contribution to the controversy over marriage and the wedding ceremony. But another complex of social problems is also introduced, namely the position of the unmarried woman in society. This is related to Almqvist's journalism on women's rights. Whereas today his attitude seems fair and justified, his contemporaries considered his ideas disruptive and destructive. Even in circles that were favorably disposed toward Almqvist there was mild protest. His enemies were soon in full outcry. *Sara Videbeck* simply created a unique sensation and provoked a good deal of polemical writing.

"Sara Videbeck literature" became a current phrase, and Almqvist was repeatedly described as "the Sara Videbeck parson"; this was one more development to attract the attention

of the cathedral chapter and arouse the suspicions of the board
of Nya elementarskolan.

In the summer of 1840 Almqvist started his first great educational journey, to France and England. Officially his intention
was to study schools, but what interested him much more were
the political and social movements of the day. In Paris he was
in the very midst of revolutions. His views found an outlet
in newspaper correspondence and were also collected for *The
Causes of European Discontent* and his later political journalism
in the '40s. Almqvist recounted his experience of French life
and literature in his novel, *Gabrièle Mimanso* (1841–42). He
left Paris for England, there to paint some suggestive and
highly tendentious pictures of London in his articles on Quincy
Parriot.

Back home, Almqvist found the year 1841 very troublesome.
His productivity decreased, his skirmishes with the cathedral
chapter continued. An acute conflict also developed with the
board of Nya elementarskolan, and in the fall of the year
Almqvist was forced to retire as principal. At the age of forty-
eight he found himself in serious financial difficulties. The Liberal
press came to his rescue.

IV *In the Public Forum: Journalist and Novelist*

Aftonbladet was the Liberal daily paper to which Almqvist
contributed most of his journalistic writing, and eventually he
became a member of its staff. It had been founded in 1830 by
the enterprising politician, businessman, and cultural personality,
Lars Johan Hierta, who rapidly turned it into a power to be
reckoned with. By 1834 Hierta's newspaper already had more
postal subscribers than all the other Stockholm newspapers put
together. In fact, *Aftonbladet* was Sweden's first modern newspaper and, as such, it played an important political role. It
represented the Liberal opposition in constitutional, social,
and political questions.

Between Hierta and Almqvist there was for a long time
mutual friendship and admiration; at the beginning of the
1840s Almqvist had a great influence on *Aftonbladet*. In May
1842 when Hierta went abroad for three months, he left the

supervision of the editorial work to Almqvist. During this time, however, unfortunate circumstances led to the so-called "Almqvist affair" in July 1842.

"The affair" was the result of an unpleasant and violent newspaper debate with August Blanche, sparked off by an extremely insinuating article against Blanche. The article created a scene at the Stockholm café Strömparterren, where Blanche publicly challenged his antagonist and spat in his face. Naturally the incident attracted great attention and did not conduce to strengthening Almqvist's position in local opinion and public life.

In November 1842 the Cathedral Chapter summoned him to a personal interview in order to examine his orthodoxy and to demand an explanation concerning not only *Sara Videbeck* and *Marjam* but also *"Prästens ställning"* ("The Clergyman's Situation"). Almqvist appeared before the Chapter, and twelve questions were submitted to him which he had to answer in writing within a month. Later Almqvist published his disputes with the chapter in his *Monography*. The feud did not lead to any legal proceedings against Almqvist, but on the other hand it hardly increased his chances of an ecclesiastical career.

In 1843 and '44 the Almqvist family were living at Sanna farm near Jönköping, and he himself divided his time between there and Stockholm. To begin with, he suffered severely from an eye complaint that proved very expensive, both on account of the cost of treatment and the loss of earnings. From 1844 he contributed to *Jönköpingsbladet* which, along with *Aftonbladet,* was to be his forum during the next few years up to and including 1848. In a letter to Vendela Hebbe on June 17, 1843, Almqvist describes his psychological qualities and goes on to try to define his position in contemporary literature.

He sees himself a strange combination of imaginative power and intellect but it is this very combination that makes the various literary and political camps reject him. Young people of the day and people in general are now aiming at a *"union of imagination and intellect* with neither excluded nor either tyrannizing over the other." But long before this can be realized, says Almqvist, he himself will be dead. "Thus, as long as I live I shall be pretty lonely, only keeping company with my imagination and my intellect and I suppose I shall be laid in some

far-off grave after they have between them driven all other
friends away from me" (*Letters*, p. 173 f.).

His feeling of loneliness and abandonment is still more marked
in his correspondence with Hazelius. In these letters Almqvist
tries to defend and justify to his friend his sense of commitment
to social questions. In a letter to Hazelius, probably written
in the fall of 1844, Almqvist sums up the accusations made
against him and his defense, and shows how badly he feels
himself misunderstood:

A cold, dark cloud seems to be enshrouding my soul, and it is hard
to see how one can have the will to go on working for a while with
literary projects or in furtherance of ideas that only bring abuse in
whichever way one turns. And nevertheless that is the only thing
I can do. I may be put in prison or driven out of the country,
stripped naked, hanged or drowned, but as long as I live, every
morning when I wake, I have no other thoughts than those I have
always had and must unrelentingly develop further.—I may be
stopped by physical violence in the career which I planned for
myself as the most appropriate and the best, for instance in asserting
the restoration of religion in our country [. . .]; as I said, I may be
forcibly prevented from being a clergyman if, in that way, my
existence is made impossible for me: but then *that* is no longer my
fault; I have expressed at all events what I consider the right way
to reach my longed-for goal. (*Letters*, p. 195)

Almqvist's impassioned reaffirmation of his need to develop
and express the ideas he believes to be right seems sincere and
convincing. We certainly know that his caution and prudence
made him withdraw, destroy, and over and over again revise
important works that were offensive to the age in which he
lived. Noteworthy examples are *Amorina, Sara Videbeck*, and
The Causes of European Discontent. On the other hand, whenever he sensed the moment was ripe, he did not hesitate to
publish controversial material, even against the advice of his
friends and even if the result was unfortunate or downright
detrimental for him. This also applies to his journalism.

The sun shone, however, during the relatively happy period
he spent in Denmark in the '40s: from November 1845 to
March 1846. In Copenhagen his name was famous, and he was

looked upon as an honored and esteemed guest. Scandinavianism had become an important movement that was finding support not only within the students' unions but also in the press and in diplomatic circles: as a journalist Almqvist had committed himself to Pan-Scandinavian ideas. A lasting result of his Danish journey was the extremely prophetic and imaginative lecture, *"Om skandinavismens utförbarhet"* ("On the Practicability of Scandinavianism"), delivered in February 1846 in Copenhagen and printed that same year.

After his return to Stockholm, Almqvist became a permanent member of the editorial staff of *Aftonbladet*, and the terms of his employment (as of April 1, 1846) were extremely favorable. In this connection Hierta and the author's brother, Fridolf, had pledged themselves to try to organize and restore his finances.

Obviously, they did not succeed. The dealings in which Almqvist seems to have entangled himself grew more and more complicated, which finally led to the notorious affair with the usurer, von Scheven.

During the 1840s Almqvist wrote six novels which—compared with such masterpieces as *The Queen's Jewel* or *Sara Videbeck*— indicate a distinct decline. Some of them show a carefree, almost cynical, adaptation of the pattern of the period's popular serial novel formula, which ill accords with the theories in "On the Poetry of Facts." Still, we must remember that during these critical years Almqvist prepared for the press the last two volumes of the imperial octavo edition. He brought earlier works up to date and put the finishing touches on them (for instance, *"Songes"*). Above all, it was during the 1840s that Almqvist was writing brilliant treatises, essays, and, especially, journalistic pieces.

Almqvist's journalism is an important part of his œuvre; in quantity it is considerable, and its quality must also be described as impressive. Perceptively, he discussed most of the burning topics of the day, whether relating to literature, parliamentary reform, or foreign policy, education, or theology. What his views in these wide-ranging fields share is faith in Liberalism, and he aspires to realism in both poetry and politics. His attitude toward marriage and feminism has already been touched upon and will be discussed further in analyses of *Sara Videbeck* and

The Causes of European Discontent. Almqvist was also an active member of Reformsällskapet (the Reform Society) and frequently wrote articles in favor of parliamentary reform. He also took an active interest in foreign policy and was—as we have already seen—a great champion of Scandinavianism. As a clergyman and opponent of the cathedral chapter, he kept a competent and certainly a critical, radical eye on theological questions.

V Catastrophe and Exile. Death

During the 1840s Almqvist's finances were extremely complex. Moreover, he held no official post, and was justly bitter at having so harshly been dismissed from the principalship of Nya elementarskolan; he also had every reason to resent the failure of the government to give him the post that he deserved. The catastrophe came at last, and in 1851 Almqvist—one of the most successful writers of his day—went into exile, suspected of attempted poisoning, forgery, and theft. Suddenly, on June 11, 1851, Almqvist left Stockholm, never to see it again in his life. After a hazardous and ingenious escape through Sweden and Denmark, he arrived at Bremen, where he boarded a ship bound for New York where he arrived in August. After fourteen years in America, he returned to Europe and died in Bremen in 1866.

The obscure events of 1851 have never been satisfactorily explained. Was Almqvist guilty of the crimes with which he was charged, or not? During the early days of June 1851 rumors alleged that Almqvist had stolen promissory notes made out by himself to the usurer Captain von Scheven and also that he had tried to poison the usurer.

The police acted quickly, and a warrant was issued for Almqvist's arrest. His house was searched, and several documents of interest were found. The man at the center of the police investigation was von Scheven, according to whom promissory notes signed by Almqvist and amounting to nearly 18,000 riks dollars—an enormous sum in those days—had disappeared in May. Almqvist was said to have made out new ones for the same sum, but to have signed them "O. Almgren." When this was discovered, he changed the signature to "C. J. L. Almqvist" and promised to make out new and testified notes. There was never time for that.

In letters written at the time of his flight abroad, Almqvist denied owing any money to von Scheven. Yet, von Scheven maintained that the large sum could be partially explained by Almqvist's drawing 10,500 riks dollars in the fall of 1850, a sum that von Scheven had previously placed with wholesale dealer Johan Ludvig Strindberg, August Strindberg's uncle. Von Scheven and Strindberg agreed that Almqvist had received the money. According to the testimony of von Scheven's maid, Almqvist had also tried several times, in May and June, to poison von Scheven with arsenic mixed with spirits or oatmeal gruel.

The most incriminating evidence, in the eyes of his contemporaries and posterity as well, were the five memoranda found in his house during the search. These memoranda sketch alternative defense strategies, explanations, even counter-attacks (if Almqvist should be subjected to examination regarding the lost notes or in the event of von Scheven's death). The memoranda are sometimes difficult to decode. They are full of private abbreviations, and the handwriting is extremely hard to read. But there is no doubt that they allude to the von Scheven affair.

One memorandum, the most damning, consists of only one sheet. The upper half of this sheet contains arguments to be put to "the old man" (= von Scheven); the lower half contains arguments to present before police and court.

At the beginning of this memorandum Almqvist intends to acknowledge the promissory notes in the presence of von Scheven, and promises to stand by his obligations or issue new notes if the old gentleman will only calm down. *But*, further down on the same page, in another explanation addressed to the police and the court, he declares that he never made out any notes to von Scheven. He flatly denies everything.

Unfortunately, the juxtaposition of these two declarations, focusing the same matter differently for different audiences, does not inspire confidence. Lastly, what weighed most heavily against Almqvist was the fact that he fled from the police investigation and the trial and stayed out of the country.

As a *regimental* chaplain, the poet was subject to military law, and the verdict of the Court-Martial of Appeal against

Almqvist was recorded on September 29, 1853. It declared that "the Court-Martial of Appeal found that the evidence against Almqvist was more than half substantiated." Consequently, Almqvist could neither be acquitted nor convicted. As it was put in the record: "The matter must rest for the time being until the truth should be revealed." Since Almqvist had left the country, he was removed from his post as regimental chaplain. In the lawsuit before the Stockholm City Court, Almqvist was declared bankrupt, and as a defaulter, he was sentenced to the pillory and three years' imprisonment.

In the summer of 1851, a press campaign was launched against both Almqvist and Hierta and *Aftonbladet* as well, a campaign unprecedented in its venom. With few exceptions, Almqvist's contemporaries—friends and enemies as well—believed he was guilty.

Almqvist, then, ran away from rumors and trial: during the first stages of his escape he wrote three letters to Hierta and one to V. Stråhle, chief of the Stockholm police. In these letters he defended himself vigorously—but sometimes vaguely—against the accusations. Yet it was only on very rare occasions later that he casually touched upon these questions in his correspondence: indeed, *he never confessed to the crimes.*

In July 1851 Almqvist signed a short note to Thomander with his name, "Love," and the words "a little better than his reputation" (*Letters*, p. 217). This afterthought is perhaps Almqvist's most sincere utterance in this entire mysterious affair.

The reactions of Almqvist's contemporaries have already been considered. His adversaries indulged in an orgy of disparagement, and even Hierta and *Aftonbladet*, his own newspaper, came out against him. It is astonishing to see how by and large very few people tried to distinguish between the man and his work. Even his closest friends had some difficulty in not letting the shocking events color their opinion.

One assessment which seems particularly damaging is that of his son Ludvig in a letter to his uncle, Fridolf Almqvist. Ludvig was really afraid that his father might take it into his head to come back and defend himself against the accusations. "Papa's excuses and explanations of everything that he is suspected of with reference to the notes, are undeniably well

constructed and would be fully convincing in a novel. [. . .]
Unfortunately the most incriminating things still remain and
are there recorded in the proceedings and can certainly not
be gainsaid."[4]

In the question of Almqvist's guilt, many scholars have offered their opinion. Some have taken the stance of a public
prosecutor; others have given heartfelt appeals as counsels for
the defense.[5] But the problem is still unsolved, and the last
word remains to be said: it will no doubt be a long time before
the court of research establishes the truth and prepares to
pass judgment.

Whether guilty or not, Almqvist fled the country and stayed
in exile for the rest of his life. After traveling about America,
he finally settled in Philadelphia in February 1854 for his last
eleven years in the States.

A letter to his wife dated April 12, 1854, tells her his impressions of the new town and also gives a detailed description
of his landlady, Emma Nugent, "a fat, gray-haired, generous
little woman with quite round, extremely cheerful eyes." This
would certainly have interested Mrs. Almqvist if she had known
that on June 11, 1854, under the name of Lewis Gustawi, Almqvist was to marry Mrs. Nugent. However, he managed to keep
his bigamy secret. It was not until 1928 that this fact was
exposed by Ruben G:son Berg.[6]

It was probably Almqvist's financial situation that made him
marry Emma Nugent. It is evident that the marriage was a failure
and that he had only exchanged European discontent for an
American variety. He evidently helped with errands, entertainment, etc., in his wife's boardinghouse. We know for certain
that he spent much time reading in the city library—records have
been preserved—and he was busy collecting material for his
book, *Om svenska rim* (*On Swedish Rhymes*).

Fortunately, a great deal of Almqvist's correspondence from
America has been saved, and I shall return later to his American
letters and poems. Photographs from 1863 show the face of a
tired, tormented old man, perhaps lacking self-confidence, and
without illusions.

And then Almqvist set out on his life's last long journey. He
had left Stockholm suddenly in June 1851, and he left Emma

Nugent-Gustawi's house just as suddenly in July 1865. He managed to return to Europe; in October 1865 he was in Bremen.

The long journeys and his restless life during the years of exile bear witness to his persistent and almost unbelievable ability to survive. When Almqvist left Sweden, he was a man of almost sixty: he had worked hard and fared badly but had managed to make his escape in the nick of time. Then he crossed over to a distant, unfamiliar continent where he was deprived of his means of subsistence because of the language barrier; yet somehow he survived for fourteen years, and then managed to return to Europe for another year.

It was his longing for his family in Sweden that drove Almqvist to set out on the long journey back. His first letter from Bremen is lost, but evidently he thought it would be possible for him to return to Sweden for good, or at least to visit Sweden. Instead his panic-stricken family seems to have suggested that he should go further away, at least to England. This can be gathered from the fragment of a heartbroken letter written in the fall of 1865, from which it is clear that his motive was his longing to see his family and his horror of "having to die in unfamiliar arms" (*Letters*, p. 274).

Almqvist stayed on in Bremen where he was tolerably well provided for but, though separated from his family by only two or three days' journey, he never saw his wife and children again. He fell ill in September 1866 and was shortly afterward removed to the Bremen hospital. Fridolf came to see him, but his daughter could not get there in time. On September 26 Almqvist died, of weakness due to old age, and was buried in a pauper's grave. In 1901 his remains were taken to Sweden and placed in the Gjörwell family grave in the cemetery at Solna, near Stockholm.

CHAPTER 2

Early Literary Production

I Stylistic Exercises and Swedenborgian Poetry

ALMQVIST'S earliest experiments with poems have been described by Henry Olsson as "stylistic exercises and holiday poetry of a rather trivial kind."[1] Most are printed in the first volume of his *Collected Works.*

Almqvist's literary style before 1815 was influenced by the fashions of the eighteenth century, by the Enlightenment, sentimentality, and pre-Romanticism. Only after his conversion to Swedenborgianism did he approach the Romantics of his day with his conception of poetry and the poet's vocation.

In his essay entitled "Introduction to Dalmina" he indicated his attitude toward the two rival literary schools in Sweden: the old "Gustavian" (Classicist) and the new "Phosphoristic" (Romantic) school. Almqvist regarded the new poetry as a third kind, "whose tendency will be higher than either of the others" (*CW*, II, p. 221).

In an essay, in 1915, on the earlier works, Martin Lamm revealed the important Swedenborgian influences on Almqvist's philsophical and literary writings.[2] He borrowed the principal lines of Swedenborg's system—especially his spiritual doctrine—and also to a considerable extent his scholastic style. Lamm also points out that Almqvist never liberated himself from Swedenborgian speculation, at any rate not during the years in which he devoted himself more or less completely to philosophical writings. The practical ideas which established Almqvist's fame as a social reformer, the theory of the rehabilitation of criminals and the doctrine of marriage, were also derived from Swedenborgian impulses. Lamm also discusses the Moravian sect and its significance for Almqvist in his youth. In general, Almqvist liked to combine Moravian bridal mysticism with

31

Swedenborg's doctrine of spiritual marriages. The chief importance of the Moravian sect for Almqvist was the sustenance it provided his sentimentality. In spite of all his contacts with Romanticism, Almqvist's mysticism preserves its popular fundamental pietistic character.

We also find the poet Almqvist at work in the unfinished epic *Karmola* (1817), his first attempt to create the great popular religious poem applying Swedenborg's spiritual doctrine (and set, consequently, in both heaven and hell).

II Parjumouf *and Other Tales and Studies*

Parjumouf. Saga ifrån Nya Holland (*Parjumouf. A Tale from New Holland*) has fewer speculative features. It was published anonymously at the end of 1817; a special copy is furnished with the explanatory subtitle, *An Attempt at Lafontainizing*, which alludes to a favorite author of Almqvist's, the German manufacturer of sentimental novels, August Lafontaine.

This is the story of *Parjumouf*:

Beyond the Blue Mountains near Botany Bay in New Holland (Australia), Sariving, son of the king of the Beronguls, loves the beautiful Princess Amsaïs, daughter of the king of the Ceringals. Between the two Indian tribes is implacable enmity. In a battle between the Ceringals and the Beronguls the two lovers are separated. Amsaïs is taken prisoner by her fellow countrymen and is condemned to death. Sariving, badly wounded, is tended by his sister Parjumouf, who later sets out secretly to find Amsaïs. Through a mixture of innocence and ruse, Parjumouf manages to liberate Amsaïs and afterward brings about a reconciliation between the two previously hostile peoples.

Thus the primary theme of this tale—love between descendants of warring families—may be called a Romeo-and-Juliet motif with a happy ending. Parjumouf's personality and exploits illustrate the idea, which we find formulated in the text as the narrator suggests that "innocence in itself has a strong capacity, an innate resourcefulness of its own to accomplish great deeds" (*CW*, I, p. 331).

This subject is presented to the reader by means of a Chinese box narrative technique, in which one tale contains another.

The story of Parjumouf's deeds is told first by a nameless Indian to a French officer who, for his part, passes this story on to the guests of a rich wine merchant of Bordeaux. Here we also find the first-person narrator who finally tells the story to the reader.

Both the narrative technique and the exotic subject matter are typical of Almqvist. He frequently uses the framework story; the prime example is, of course, *The Book of the Wild Rose*. Almqvist's interest in faraway countries is well known. He stressed it himself many times. "Even the geographical names of cities and provinces made on me an impression which created new worlds in my imagination," he says in the delightful little story, *"Kartans behag"* ("The Charm of the Map"; *CW*, IV, p. 246).

It was Rousseau's and the eighteenth century's conception of the noble savage that was behind Almqvist's description of Parjumouf. She is akin to such other beautiful and heroic "female savages" as, for instance, Chateaubriand's Atala.

Innocence, grace, and shyness but also resourcefulness, presence of mind, and resolution are qualities characteristic of Parjumouf. She also heralds a long line of young Almqvist heroines such as Tintomara, Schems-el-Nihar, Brita in "Skällnora Mill," and Gabrièle Mimanso.

Parjumouf was Almqvist's first major step in the field of fiction, even if it is a far cry from *Murnis* and even farther from *Amorina*. But in the Swedish literature of the period it stands out as a charmingly exotic idyll, and it seems that in the 1830s Almqvist had firmly intended to insert *Parjumouf* into *The Book of the Wild Rose*.

The Romantics' artistic fairy tale, incorporating symbolically interpreted folk material, was attempted by Almqvist in *"Guldfågel i paradis"* ("Goldbird in Paradise," 1821)—a variant of the Rip Van Winkle motif—and in "Rosaura" (1822), "the story of the wings of charm." These tales were also published anonymously, but Almqvist included them later in the imperial octavo edition of *The Book of the Wild Rose*.

"Goldbird in Paradise" was severely criticized in the press, and Almqvist defended his work, notably in letters to Palmblad and Atterbom. Almqvist had come into close contact with the

Romantic phalanx about 1820. Together with Lorenzo Hammar-skjöld, he edited the periodical *Hermes* (1821–22), and there he published, among other things, the two important essays, *"Om brottsliges behandling"* ("On the Treatment of Criminals") and *"Om enheten av epism och dramatism. En aning om den poetiska fugan"* ("On the Unity of Epic and Drama. A Conception of the Poetic Fugue"). In 1821 he began to correspond with Atterbom. This correspondence continued through the following year, was then interrupted for a decade and resumed in 1831. In the middle of the 1830s the correspondence was particularly frequent; in the spring of 1840 farewell letters were exchanged. The letters that have been preserved are extremely interesting, for of all the authors whom Almqvist befriended, only Atterbom appeared to be his equal. In the letters we see a professional commenting upon and presenting his own work to a colleague, asking for an opinion and giving good advice. The collaboration of the two Swedish Romantics bears modest comparison with that of Goethe and Schiller.

In the years around 1820 Almqvist was occupied with three major projects which often figure in his correspondence and to which he and his friends attached great expectations. They were the great organization plan for Manhemsförbundet, and also *Murnis* and *Amorina*. *Informative Documents Regarding the History of Manhemsförbundet* was published in 1820 but did not become the success they had hoped for (cf. above p. 15), and the two works of fiction were not published at all during this period.

III   Murnis

The manuscript of the remarkable work, *Murnis*, once finished in December 1819, was studied by admiring friends: "We have read *Murnis*. That is the well-spring. When we are thirsty we go to the source," the enthusiastic J. A. Hazelius writes in 1820.[3] But the first and most interesting version was not printed until 1960. In 1845 the revised work was published—with many alterations and omissions—under the title *De dödas sagor* (*The Tales of the Dead*). This second version was reprinted with further slight alterations in 1850 under the title, *Murnis*, in the imperial octavo edition of *The Book of the Wild Rose*.

While working on *Murnis*, Almqvist himself called his work partly an "Idyllion," partly "a kind of erotic epic in fifteen books" (*Letters*, pp. 22 and 30)—an epic in prose, we must add. In a letter from his period in America, Almqvist characterizes his work more concisely as "an Epic in XV Books, in prose." It might rather be called a tale, often presented in rhythmic and lyric prose with features reminiscent of Ossianic poetry. With reference to form as well as subject, *Murnis* has links with Celtic material, and this is still more marked in the third version (1850), in which the narrator calls the work a *mabinogion*, using the Celtic title of a series of Welsh myths and legends from the fourteenth century. Thus, in form and style, *Murnis* is truly a Romantic work related to several genres: the religious epic, visionary poetry, the short story, the *Entwicklungsroman*, and not least, the myth, the folk tale, and the artistic fairy tale.

The plot is roughly as follows:

A man is betrothed to his beloved, but God separates the two lovers on earth, and the woman is drowned. The man is forced to endure a long penance on earth. When he dies, he goes to Heaven and is reunited with his beloved. They rise to the Isle of Murnis, the most paradisical part of Heaven. Here—like all those who have loved each other truly on earth—they continue their life together after death, rising toward higher and higher forms of existence.

Thus, *Murnis* is enacted in two worlds: in the early mythical Middle Ages and in a timeless paradise of happiness after death, in celestial climes.

Added to this central plot are tales of other loving couples' happy reunions in Heaven after a separation by cruel events on earth. These couples devote themselves mainly to vigorous erotic activity, heavenly in its innocence but definitely secular in character. This conception of life after death derives, as is well known, from Swedenborg's doctrine of the spiritual world, a doctrine of great importance to Almqvist. This also explains the title given to the second version: *The Tales of the Dead.* The same version has the subtitle, "*Celiorama,*" which Almqvist himself defines as "a sort of view of Heaven." Since such rich life awaits the believer after death, it is easy to understand that, in Almqvist's work and belief, death never seems terrifying but instead often possesses a dangerous appeal. We shall have several opportunities to return to Almqvist's remarkable religious and ideological views on this subject (e.g., p. 85). There is, by the way, a remarkable likeness between Almqvist and William Blake, especially in *Murnis* and in some *songes*, a likeness due no doubt to their common interest in Swedenborg and in Ossian.

An omniscient narrator tells the story, often apostrophizing the fictitious character and sometimes also the reader.

The narrator's account in the third person (narrative, comment, etc.) comprises roughly 60 percent of the entire text; the rest is direct speech by fictitious persons in monologue and dialogue. I shall return to the distribution of epic and dramatic elements in relation to *Amorina* and particularly *The Queen's Jewel*.

In a few of the chapters there are traces of a framework tale, an epic situation in which the narrator refers to Philomela, the nightingale, she being the one who, as he says, actually pours out the whole story in song.[4] I must point out, however, that this initial device may not deliberately have been sustained but only intended perhaps as a hint, a touch—quite in keeping with the predominant Romantic aesthetics of the fragmentary or the unfinished.

Repetition and variation are conspicuous features in *Murnis*. They are evident not only in the composition (the motif, "reunion of the faithful lovers after adverse fortune," runs through the whole of *Murnis*) but also stylistically (parallelism and repetitions abound).

Antiquated words and word forms are common. In this first version Almqvist is also quite outspoken on sexual matters and describes in detail, with pious desire and chaste lust, the divine and uninhibited lovemaking.

In the revision of the later (printed) versions, however, passages that were too openly erotic were cut out. In a letter to Atterbom, mentioned above, Almqvist optimistically offers *Murnis* as a kind of serial story for *Poetisk kalender* (*The Poetic Calendar*), but this idea came to nothing. In the same letter he comments on the possibility of presenting a naked Beauty in a Romantic, *Christian, holy, cool, pure, sound* sense [. . .]: then instead of the lust and desire that it rouses as a pagan Nudity, it would here, on the contrary, evoke in the spectator the cool chastity of holy innocence [. . .] It is in such a spirit (with a new form, content, and coloring of its own) that the literary piece is written which I am now offering to you. (*Letters,* p. 31)

In other words, the innocence he aims at here is different from the innocence he describes in *Parjumouf.*

The vocabulary covers a wide range of colors; it is extremely Romantic: jasper, emeralds, topazes, rubies, diamonds, purple, etc.

The imagery is rich and varied; metaphor predominates. Like most Romantics, Almqvist was fond of synaesthesia, and in *Murnis* there are several ingeniously executed examples, for instance the following: "And a shimmer of purple sent its fragrance like a veil down over them and a song resounded through the shimmer" (*Murnis,* 1960, p. 150).

We see that the synaesthesia quoted contains visual, auditory, and olfactory components.

Thus, in Almqvist's first great work of prose fiction, the poet experiments with genres, subject, composition, and style. His composition generally builds on contrasts, revealing greater artistic planning than his earlier works.[5] His language is flexible; he tries to combine high and low, giving expression to heavenly piety as well as sexual pleasure.

In Almqvist's mixture of genres, of subjects (religion and sexuality), and in his mixture of sensations characteristic of synaesthesia, we see demonstrated the concern of Romantic aesthetics with mixture and variation: in other words, its notion of the universality of poetry.

IV Amorina

The second great work from Almqvist's youth, *Amorina,* like *Murnis,* did not reach the public until late. The printing of *Amorina* was almost completed in 1822, but the author destroyed the sheets. It was not until seventeen years later, in 1839, that *Amorina* appeared in print, complete and also revised.

Amorina is far more mature and significant than *Murnis* or

Parjumouf: Almqvist had made enormous progress artistically. Nevertheless, *Amorina* is a work of glaring colors and strong effects. The following short summary traces the plot of the later version.

Twin brothers Wilhelm and Rudman Falkenburg love the same young woman, Henrika, who eventually turns out to be their sister. She has grown up at the vicarage in Danderyd where her mother had gone to live after marrying the grotesque vicar, Dr. Libius. The noble general Wilhelm Falkenburg wins Henrika's love, and after Wilhelm has committed suicide (owing to a misunderstanding), Henrika gives birth to his son. She is also coveted by the evil brother, Rudman Falkenburg, from whom she escapes only with difficulty. Under the name of Amorina, Henrika wins a great reputation as a preacher and miracleworker; her manner is impressive, but highstrung and insane.

Johannes, a mad and bloodthirsty murderer, is allied with the villainous Rudman. Both Amorina and Johannes are imprisoned by society as criminals. Rudman goes mad with remorse and fright at supernatural events (whereby a family curse is fulfilled). Johannes escapes and tries to liberate Amorina, who turns out to be his cousin. He fails, however, and it is Amorina's father's ghost who liberates her. Johannes commits suicide after murdering a great many people to slake his thirst for blood, and Amorina and Rudman are drowned on a boat trip. In this way the family curse is finally fulfilled.

We see that Almqvist gathered together some of the most popular and blood-curdling motifs in world literature: the incest motif, the triangle motif, the confusion motif, and the motif of the hatred between brothers, to mention only a few of the most conspicuous. Olle Holmberg, who has studied the prototypes of *Amorina*, sums up: "All that Almqvist read in his youth comes together in *Amorina* for a stormy shareholders' meeting."[6]

Nevertheless, in spite of its many clichés and blood-curdling excesses, *Amorina* remains strangely alive. The language is expressive and flexible, and the absurd events are animated with realistic details; regardless of the situations—which are in many respects ghostly—the characters seem to be flesh-and-blood figures. The fair, high-strung principal character is nicely balanced by the wretched murderer, Johannes, and the comical, grotesque Dr. Libius. The latter is one of the few scurrilous figures of Swedish Romanticism to deserve admission to an E. T. A. Hoffmann style gallery of grotesques.

Amorina is also a religious work. It was influenced by the ideas of the Manhem plan, and the heroine is an imitator of Christ. She is a Christian, truly religious, philanthropic, and self-sacrificing: a contrast to the clergyman, Dr. Libius, who is hardhearted and selfish. *Amorina* also provides plenty of religious symbolism, and its conception of death is the same as Swedenborg's. Lamm has stressed that the fundamental symbolic idea of the work is that the principal character—through her sufferings, her preaching, and her death—shall be the redeemer of her family in the same way as Christ was the redeemer of humankind.[7]

Ill-fated love, wild comical detail, and caustic satire all mingle together in *Amorina*. But the work also reveals a strong interest in social issues in its effort to understand the psychology of deranged and criminal individuals and to regard them as the diseased victims of environment. Here is the same line of reasoning as that pursued in the impressively modern theoretical essay, "On the Treatment of Criminals" (1821), in which Almqvist declares that every criminal is a sick person who should be healed, not punished.

Ninety percent of *Amorina* is *direct speech*, i.e., monologues or dialogues: that which is said is appended directly to the names of the persons in about the same way as in a dramatic dialogue. The narrator's epic account is only 10 percent of the text.

Almqvist called *Amorina* "a whole of alternating dramatic and epic form" or a *poetic fugue*, which to him meant a synthesis of epic and drama. He developed these thoughts further in the essay entitled "On the Unity of Epic and Drama. A Conception of the Poetic Fugue." Here Almqvist sums up: "the fugue is the whole expressed in musical art," and "the unity of epic and drama can be called the *poetic* fugue" (*CW*, II, p. 555).

Almqvist's contemporaries spoke of *Amorina* as a "tragicomedy" or "a novel in dramatic form." In an important letter of 1863, however, Almqvist classifies *Amorina* in plain language

as a "Romance," by which he means *novel*.[8] In fact, this is
natural, considering that Romanticism viewed the novel as a
higher unity of genres, comprising lyric poetry and drama as
well as epic. One recalls Friedrich Schlegel's famous words:
*"Ich kann mir einen Roman kaum anders denken als gemischt
aus Erzählung, Gesang und anderen Formen."*[9]

But there is still another type of novel that may have influenced Almqvist: namely, the dramatic or dialogue novel, a
genre which in the last decades of the eighteenth century attracted much attention in Germany but was also represented in
England in the novels of Thomas Love Peacock.

Particularly in the area of this mixture of epic and drama,
Amorina is strikingly original and full of experiments with form.
This combining is done in a few other works by Almqvist,
especially in *The Queen's Jewel* (more than 60 percent of which
is dramatic dialogue). *Karmola*, written in his youth, and the
late novel, *Amalia Hillner*, are also noteworthy examples. But
in no other work does Almqvist let the dramatic presentation
dominate the epic as it does in *Amorina*.

In the epic sections the narrator appears as a generally
omniscient figure whereas naturally he disappears during the
monologue and dialogue passages. But in the actual transitions
between epic and dramatic form, of course, one is aware of
the narrator's presence. An ingenious mixture of epic narrative
and dramatic dialogue is used by Almqvist at the end of the
second book, at which point Amorina discovers that her beloved
Wilhelm has committed suicide. It is an extremely thrilling
moment: the reader (but not Amorina) knows that Wilhelm
has taken his own life at their meeting place. Amorina first
sees him from a distance and says:

"Isn't that him I see over there [. . .] I am coming as to a splendid
party, all the air is quivering around me like a silver veil. Has he
fallen asleep down there during his play with the roses and the
sword? Wake up, wake up! I don't know whether my blue jacket
is too thin or the air too cold—I don't know, but I am trembling—it
may be because I am so happy—"

She came nearer, she came right up to him, and— (*CW*, X, p. 189 f.)

At the end of her monologue Amorina sees Wilhelm lying stretched out as if he were resting. Then her monologue is interrupted and the narrator steps in, using the epic preterite, leading the young woman nearer and nearer to the dead man. An effective dash brings the second book to an end. After her expectant and anxious monologue, filled with sinister forebodings which she does not yet comprehend, comes the narrator's final unfinished sentence. Hence, the end of the narrative fades away like a film with a final scene that recedes and disappears before the hint of alarm on the heroine's face has become certainty.

This is an excellent illustration of Almqvist's theory, presented in 1835 in the aesthetic essay, "*Dialog om sättet att sluta stycken*" ("Dialogue on How to Finish Pieces"), in which the readers themselves are asked to become contributors to the work, to let it "go on and on in unlimited inventions." This is a form of aesthetics that is not only very Romantic but also very modern.

The entire composition of *Amorina* is clearly outlined in a prophecy and a carefully constructed ghost scene in the third book. The symbolic arrangement of the scene provides a concise summary of the plot, an exposition and a glimpse into the future. This scene can be said to epitomize the entire novel just as the famous pantomime in *The Queen's Jewel* reflects the whole book. There are throughout *Amorina* parallel scenes and re-current themes that help strengthen the composition and accentuate its unity. Almqvist employs another device, the recapitulation of certain episodes, almost creating a novel within the novel. While Amorina's reputation as a wonder-worker is at its high, she meets Petrus, the schoolmaster, who initiates a patronizing conversation with her without knowing who she is. It now appears that our schoolmaster is writing Amorina's history, for he now presents a summary of it to his sister. Apart from the irony of the situation (he does not realize that one of his listeners is the venerable subject of his legend biography), this re-capitulation of events has an amusing effect, accentuating the unity of the composition. At the same time this study of Amorina's life bears witness to her reputation and importance, contributing to the illusion of reality in the character.

A variant, or rather a contrast, to the above incident is to be found in IV:7, in which the court of appeal unfeelingly pre-

sents reports on Amorina from quite another angle: the attitude
of official Sweden toward a criminal.

In the second version Almqvist also sharpens the focus of
composition with an introduction by a fictitious editor, added
in 1839. This editor tells how he found the manuscript of
Amorina through mysterious circumstances: he reflects on it,
explains it, and publishes it. This device follows a popular
preference: suffice it to recall E. T. A. Hoffmann's fictitious
editors and narrative framework technique, and of course Almqvist's predilection for the framework narrative device employed in *The Book of the Wild Rose*. The editor's analytic
and comparative argument, especially regarding the murderer
Johannes, is reminiscent of the sensible and somewhat circumstantial Herr Hugo. On the other hand, there is a touch
of Richard Furumo in the formulation of the ideas: "Does that
mean that the sharp point of a rapier is put to the most sensitive
nerve of humanity?"

As a rule, however, the editor's narration is pedantic and
devoid of humor, with a dash of academic arrogance. The
whole fictitious character of the editor presents an effective
contrast to the highly dramatic subject matter and the sanguinary
events of the manuscript.

How does the narrator portray human beings? I shall restrict
my attention to the examination of one person, in his way the
most striking: Dr. Libius.

The editor's preface portrays Libius ironically: "Though he
is kindhearted and humane, he is nevertheless, in my opinion,
a little rough; as he is often bitingly humorous, one practically
dies laughing, but he is never witty in the light, winged genre"
(*CW*, X, p. 20).

In the sequel, Libius—like the others—characterizes himself
largely by his direct speech and actions, requiring little comment
from the narrator. This mode of exposition is of course that
of drama but also of fiction (in dialogue); it also incidentally
anticipates the point of view of the modern scenic novel.

On his very first appearance, Libius assumes an unpleasant
and heavy-handed manner, accented by his highly imaginative
use of invective.

In the second book there is a memorable scene in which

Libius meets the wretched murderer Johannes, bloodstained, on a lonely forest path. Johannes is heartbroken and asks for help; he wants to know if he is lost forever. But the hard-hearted clergyman quickly dodges the question with pseudo-scientific theological and sophistic arguments. Previously it had been possible to regard the absurdly naïve and smugly autocratic Libius as a crude, genial ruffian, but now the comic element acquires a satirical edge. When he meets Johannes, he reveals his character. From a stylistic point of view, his theological explanations to Johannes are very telling. Libius's speech usually fluctuates between coarse colloquial thundering abuse and a sermonizing vibrato articulating a sequence of complex pseudo-scientific sentences in which the words have completely taken control of the thoughts.

The clergyman's answer, that Johannes is lost, ends with a little joke; it shows Libius's indifference to human problems; the inexorable but absurd logic characterizes him well, and in his parody of officialese and all its mysteries, Almqvist shows his mettle in a manner suggestive of "Ormus and Ariman." It is worth noting that this scene also presents a practical example of the Romantic conception of humor; Almqvist himself emphasized that the scene exemplifies "the kind of humor that is current here."[10]

In the fourth book the vicarage of Danderyd is burned down, and Dr. Libius dies in the fire.

Prototypes of Dr. Libius have been located by scholars in the works of Shakespeare, Bellman, and Jean Paul.[11] Shakespeare's Falstaff has been discussed in this connection, but Libius is more gruesome and more demonic.

Perhaps the most characteristic quality of *Amorina* is its *intensity*. Its argument *against* society and *in favor of* the celestial is strong, and there is an intensity in its characterization, its humor and tragedy, in its choice of words and generally in its style. As an attempt to master and mix several genres, in the spirit of Romanticism, *Amorina* is unique in Swedish literature. As an attempt to brandish the tip of the rapier—in defense of the outcast and the criminal—*Amorina* has few precursors.

Unfortunately, it was not published in 1823; if it had been,

Almqvist's writing might not have been checked at the outset, and both Swedish literature and his career might have taken a different turn.

CHAPTER 3

Toward the Book of the Wild Rose

I   *A Poetic Universal Plan:* The Tears of Beauty

*A*MORINA, then, was destroyed and Almqvist abandoned his
plans for a civil service career; instead he moved to Värmland to lead the idealized life of a peasant. During these years
he conceived a great new plan that he described in a letter to
his Manhem brother Anders Berg on June 12, 1824:

A plan has begun to take form in me for a task that I cannot
describe to you. If I die soon, the odds and ends will lie there and
be trampled under foot; but if I live for some time there will be
a Whole that includes the Whole in the *full* sense of the word. What
you have seen of my work so far (*Murnis, Amorina* and sundry prose
works) are in fact organic parts that will belong to this Whole. This
sounds strange since much of it is heterogeneous lying there frag-
mented now. Nevertheless it has its unity which will, please God,
become apparent. I assure you that I sincerely wish to finish this
task before I die. For this work I have no other plan to follow than
the stuff of my whole being which longs to record its view of the
world therein. If I am harmonious, the whole work will be so too:
if I am a stick or a blade of grass the whole work will be hay which
will soon wither and perish in the universal oblivion down here and
will then do no harm: in my second life I shall then take this blade
of grass with me and shall get a flower from it.—This work has no
limit to its tales other than the history of the world, no limit to its
descriptions other than the Universe. I know no more. It begins with
night and despair, as was my state during a long period of my life
(I do not know if I have told you that). It begins with night and
chaos like the Creation, for it is intended to relate the whole of
history from the beginning. *Murnis* and the rest will only come
toward the end of the whole story; though not at the very end.
Apart from the general idea of the plan, I have up to the present
completed only the first four pieces which are called: "*The Tears of*

45

Beauty," "Semiramis," "Ormus and Ariman," and *"Derceto."* Pieces
in prose (what people call theses) will also have their places in the
Whole, since they are organically as necessary as the poetical pieces.
Each piece has a life so constituted that it can be read on its own
(it has its own individual temper; and it can also be read in the
context of the Whole which is its principal purpose). This is no
strange thing in itself. An acacia hedge is, if you will, merely an
acacia hedge, complete in itself: but it is also a part of the world.
(*Letters*, p. 61 f.)

Here Almqvist had sketched out a poetic universal plan, intended to include both the works he had already completed
and his future production. In the letter he presents his plan as a
gigantic survey of the history of humanity beginning with the
Creation; he was never to give this notion up. It was certainly
a long time before it appeared in print—nine years later in
the first volume of *The Book of the Wild Rose* (cf. above,
p. 16)—and it was to be modified in several respects. But it is
always present in some way or other, and with its mighty
aspiration toward the Whole, it is a beautiful and characteristic
expression of the Romantic view of the universality of poetry.

The four pieces that Almqvist describes in his letter as
complete were not printed until 1839 in the imperial octavo
edition of *The Book of the Wild Rose*; however, I shall deal
with the most important of them here.

The most striking is the lovely romantic myth of the Creation,
"Skönhetens tårar" ("The Tears of Beauty"), which presents
a dualistic conception of the world through imaginative story
and profound symbol. Richard Furumo relates his dream of
the Creation: a beautiful and divinely charming young woman
is pursued through empty space by a giant:

When her eyes could see no further help, when she already felt
that the giant's arm almost seized the veil around her shoulders,
then she sank down trembling, lost, half-conscious. But the giant,
seized with pity, in order to prevent the fair girl from falling,
put his hard hand in front of her head—alas, his fingers were sharp!
they hurt the unfortunate girl's fine forehead: a drop of her blood
ran down her forehead and mingled with the tears in her eyes. One
of these tears fell from her eyelids when sighing, expiring, she closed

her orbs. This tear of beauty fell through infinite space—the lower part of it was blood, but the upper part was tear-water.

The lower element, the blood of the tear, was heavy and wanted to descend; but the clear beautiful water, the last part of the expiring beauty; this upper part of the tear, was light, wanted to ascend to the eye, back to its origin. For that reason Astarte—that was the name of the heavenly, pursued nymph—for that reason Astarte's tear was suspended in space and is so still.

This tear is the world in which you live, my friend. (*CW*, XIII, p. 45 f.)

This myth of the Creation is a natural overture to a work that is to relate "the whole of history from the beginning." Of this little tale Almqvist himself has said that its fundamental idea comprises "all the *Wild Rose* writings in embryo. [. . .] The joy of *Wild Rose* stands above sorrow and tears and in that sense it has the whole element of tears beneath as a substratum and a shadowy foundation" (*CW*, XV, p. 350).

"Semiramis," the tale that comes next, describes how the Assyrian empire is founded. Beautiful Semiramis and her misfortunes symbolize how goodness and beauty fight a losing battle against the evil on earth.

II   *"Ormus and Ariman"*

The most important of these descriptions of primeval times, however, is the ingenious tale of "Ormus and Ariman." The sequence of the first pieces in the imperial octavo edition of *The Book of the Wild Rose* still shows evidence of the original working plan: in "The Tears of Beauty" the creation of the world is related, in "Semiramis" the origin of things and beings in the tear of beauty, and the foundation of the first empire in the world, Assyria. With "Ormus and Ariman," Almqvist intended to describe the moral organization of the earth, the origin of state authority and politics.[1]

"Ormus and Ariman" can be classified as a philosophical and satirical tale. It purports to be told by Richard Furumo (who calls it a "moral, geographic, and political tale"), and an introduction and conclusion place it within the *Wild Rose* frame.

The narrator presents the Persian myth of Ormus and Ariman,

which assumes two supreme beings. Almqvist's source seems to
have been Görres's *Mythengeschichte der asiatischen Welt*
(1810), but the material has been subjected to strange transformations. The two supreme beings, Ormus (who is good) and
Ariman (who is evil), clash in a horrible conflict. Benevolent
but naïve, Ormus, from his palace on the moon, rules the earth
in a highly authoritarian, bureaucratic fashion. His secretariat
provides the narrator with a satirical replica of the bureaucracy
of his time. Ariman, dark and demonic but wise, protests against
the lunar bureaucracy and urges Ormus to settle among the
people and try to understand and lead them. A bitter quarrel
ensues, and Ormus adds Ariman to his list of suspects. From
Ormus's secretariat the most exacting edicts and decrees are
issued, including the celebrated pedestrian regulations. This
ordinance emphasizes that all citizens are free to use any street
they choose. *However*, so that no confusion or crowding may
arise, all citizens must specify annually (when filing their taxes)
which streets they intend to use during the coming year and
enclose an appropriate application. The authorities will then,
"at their own discretion, confirm everybody's walking habits
during the year." The stamp duty paid for the permit will be
used to pay the salary of the supervisors who will have to be
posted at every street corner in order "to make sure that every
citizen walks along his street and to demand payment of a fine
if he digresses" (*CW*, XIII, p. 224 f.).

Deadly accurate stylistic parody and high comedy combine to
create a famous satire that is frightening in its timelessness.

Another ordinance is the "Rescript on the Appointment of
a Regent," which strikes us as an urgent matter in the Europe
of the 1820s, in the wake of Napoleon and the Holy Alliance.
Every regent rules by the Grace of Ormus and must be obeyed.

But if, while one person is sitting on the throne (cf. section IV),
another person in the kingdom rises up and makes a disturbance: if
he does not succeed, he shall be considered a criminal of the worst
kind and one of Ariman's villains; but if he gets the better of the
former and drives him from the throne, then shall you pay homage
to the victor, he being the one who has by us been given the power
to rule over you, and then shall you call the defeated man Ariman's
villain and treat his as such. (*CW*, XIII, p. 226)

This is undeniably the most artless and at the same time the most cynical of the regulations.

But Ormus's regulations were not accepted on earth without opposition. He soon found that,

at night. . . . At night an amazing genius of many and various shapes flew about the earth. Without plan, without purpose, without any method, it came, left, worked, and succeeded.

When for instance Ormus gave some white flower buds purple sap for a special purpose, which he explained to them carefully: so that their opening white petals in this way should acquire shades of red, which would, according to all calculations, highly embellish them. Then at night, in the light of the stars, a genius passed by, quick as a ghost: his whole shape was not seen, only teeth and lips, in the form of a man's laughing mouth. As this frightened the tender flowers, their fibers turned cold as ice, and the purple sap given by Ormus became blue-black; several delicate fibers in the flowers burst, and the transformed sap spurted over the petals in streaks without any pattern, but only as the sudden fright had forced it.

In the morning, if observers had looked, they would have been amazed! The result of Ormus's directions was not to be seen—but the rose was beautiful (with these new unexpected streaks so nobly beautiful that the observer could not tear himself away from looking at it). [. . .] However, the transformation had not always been what we would call successful; many a time the agitation had been so great as to make the tender flowers burst and lie withering away on the ground. Could a ghost command this kind of charm? Could it create beauty? (*CW*, XIII, p. 228 f.)

Thus the "chaos god of the life of instinct" protests against the "red tape god of standardization"[2]; this makes the tale something much more than one of our most brilliant satires upon the pomposity and bureaucracy of the civil service. Part of the material originates, of course, with Almqvist's own experience as a civil servant; but the satire affects only one of the parties: namely, the benevolent but (unconsciously) extremely cynical Ormus. By combining Ormus with the irrational, demonic, anarchistic Ariman, Almqvist deepens the tale's perspective. As a contrast to strictly formal beauty, the bright order of day, he juxtaposes nocturnal laughter and magic and a lovely ghost who brings on sudden transformations and mutations—which are beautiful but at times mortal. As a contrast to the conscious, he exhibits the subconscious: Freud, as it were, before his day.

The tale concludes with a despairing commentary by Richard Furumo in the epic ending at the Hunting Seat:

> Why is the good man stupid—
> Why is the wise man evil—
> Why is everything a tattered rag—

The opposition between Ormus and Ariman is illuminating for an understanding of Almqvist's life and writing. Here the conflicting tendencies in the author's own character are revealed. In a letter to Vendela Hebbe (June 17, 1843), Almqvist spoke about the Ariman and Ormus qualities of his own character (i.e., the imaginative and rational sides) (*Letters*, p. 174).

III *Romantic Medieval Novels*

The medieval novels *Cypressen* (*The Cypress*; never published by Almqvist) and *Hermitaget* (*The Hermitage*; printed in 1833 in *The Book of the Wild Rose*) also date from his Värmland period. It was Sir Walter Scott and the historical novel that provided the model; Almqvist already knew Scott before his Värmland journey, according to a letter from J. A. Hazelius in which Almqvist reminds him of "the little chamber where we read Walter Scott together" (October 7, 1823).

The Cypress relates the life of Sigfrid, a fifteenth-century knight who is trying to release himself from the pact with the Devil that his mother concluded on his account. A demonic mixture of humor and horror with elements derived from Swedish folk tales, *The Cypress* is of great autobiographical interest. Thus, while Sir Walter Scott may have furnished the model for the setting and the genre, the German Romantic novels and tales were also a major influence, particularly the writings of E. T. A. Hoffmann. The old tale offers significant possibilities of allegorical and symbolic interpretation: in a deeper sense, it deals with the problem of evil.

The Hermitage, like *The Cypress*, reveals an element of

folk tale, but here the subject is historical: it is taken from *The Chronicle of Erik*. The novel is enacted in the thirteenth century, the time of the supremacy struggle within the Folkung dynasty, and in the forefront is King Valdemar who is torn between Queen Sofia and Princess Jutta. The scene is set partly in Sweden, partly in Scotland. However, it is not the historical course of events that is predominant in the book; the actual events are treated as rather irrelevant incidents. In many respects, *The Hermitage* is a modern novel about marriage which, however, concludes with Father Amaury's remarkable doctrine of celibacy.[3] The style varies between the realism described in its setting and some magnificent examples of Romantic irony; deliberate anachronisms are introduced to afford a dizzying sense of illusion: the people of the thirteenth century can be shown gathered around a tea table in a pose more or less suggestive of the Romantic circle of Uppsala in the 1820s.

On one occasion, when Queen Sofia is meditating in solitude, she expresses the Romantic dream of *"Gesamtkunstwerk,"* formulating the notion of the undivided senses and the union of all the arts:

It is not right that our senses should be said to be five; man is one in everything, he has only *one* sense. But a fine and powerful sense notices everything in a fivefold way. In a wonderful piece of music not only do melodious waves reach the ear—. [. . .] The music finally includes the perception of touch, which is not the fifth of the senses but the mysterious generating source of the sense proper, in which every note struck reaches the ear as a tone, the eye as a shape, the nose in a sweet breath, and grows into a delicious fruit for man's mouth. . . . (*CW*, V, p. 180 f.)

Besides the Romantic features we can discover other elements in the novel. Erik Lindström finds traits of the sentimental novel, with Richardson and Rousseau as its most prominent founders; he also sees a direct connection between the doctrine of Father Amaury and that of Father Aubry in Chateaubriand's *Atala*.[4]

IV   *A Life Above the Life of Questions*

After returning from Värmland, Almqvist endured some difficult years before he was permanently employed as a teacher and principal of Nya elementarskolan. This period has been considered one of the dreariest in Almqvist's life. That he regarded the world and the order of things as a tattered rag is evident from several letters and drafts. In *"Gudahataren"* ("The Man Who Hated God")—printed much later in 1839 as a sixth book of "The Hunting Seat"—he discusses the theodicy problem, and the only way of solving this problem is for the questioner to try to elevate himself above the problems into mysticism: "he who does not have a life above the life of questions has no life."

In the years following his Värmland period, he probably also wrote the fine lyric prose monologue, *"Skaldens natt"* ("The Poet's Night"), printed in 1838 in volume XI of *The Book of the Wild Rose*. It is a dream, an ecstatic vision: it is the very moment of devotion to God that is described. From his elevated position above human beings, the poet looks at the great problems, as it were, from above and outside:

I heard the thunder rise on the clouds, and the frightened firmament spread out its wings over the earth, trembling. But I smiled and said: The flash of lightning is beautiful. [. . .]
    I saw flowers bud, I saw flowers wither. I painted.
    I saw children grow into boys and girls. I saw the girls flourish and grow into women, beautiful as the roses of life; I then saw them grow older, wither and pass away. I saw the boys grow into men, I heard them talk wisely and sharply. I then saw them grow older, I saw them become pale and grey. But I went on being what I am and have been: nothing.
    I only paint. (*CW*, VIII, p. 347 f.)

But the poet longs to return to human beings and wants to be one of them, and the prose poem ends in a prayer: "God— my God—this is my last prayer to you: let me also wither and die, like the others."

As has already been mentioned, "The Poet's Night" is supposed to have been written in the years following the Värmland period; at that time his longing for communion with God and a quiet life as a poet often recurs in his works. The final prayer, on the other hand (as has been suggested), may have been added at the 1838 printing in connection with Almqvist's changed attitude toward his fellow beings and reality (see further p. 97).

In any case, "The Poet's Night" is a very important psychological document bearing on Almqvist's intimate life. He has stressed this himself in a letter: "This very piece, though short, explains my earlier inner history best. [...] For, many years ago, I experienced an inner state of much struggle, but God turned everything into inner peace" (*Letters*, p. 140 f.).

The little drama, *Ferrando Bruno* (probably written in 1826), is about a young man named Ferrando Bruno who, after being jilted, searches for truth, eventually in the black book. In order to reach out further he drowns himself in the Adriatic Sea and awakens in the spiritual world. Here the drama begins. In defiance of God, Bruno searches for Satan whom he regards as the evil but nonetheless powerful creator and preserver of the world; this is how Ferrando solves the theodicy problem. On his wanderings in the spiritual world, he comes to the Archangel Michael, who has defeated Satan, and the Archangel leads Ferrando to a spring in the waters of which he is to see Satan. The image Ferrando sees in the spring, however, is his own, and at last he understands the Swedenborgian doctrine that we create our own devil within ourselves and that the Satan he has been searching out is a part of his own self. Thereupon Ferrando is redeemed and comes to God.

Thus we have once more been reminded of Almqvist's doubts, perplexing problems, and longing for peace: for a life *above* the life of questions.

V *The Poetic Traveler*

All the while he was pursuing his studies of the spiritual world, Almqvist was also moving into real life. In the spring and summer of 1827, he took the first of his long holiday journeys in Sweden. His destination was Östergötland, and we can read all about it in his letters to his family. The detailed gay accounts show us a bit of everyday Swedish reality, rendered enthusiastically with the discoverer's infectious joy. In 1829 the holiday tour took him to Västergötland, in 1836 and '37 to Småland and Scania. In a letter from America dated August 7,

1854, he sums up his traveling life with this comment on his journeys in Sweden:

> With the exception of the places in the north I have been in almost every Swedish town, I have an accurate memory of all the provinces and classes of people there—and to what purpose one may well ask. What had I got to do in Wimmerby, in Westervik, in Carlscrona, in Örebro, in Linde, in Fahlun, in . . . Strictly speaking, nothing! And yet I cannot say that it has been pointless. Everything has had its consequences and so will the present journeys some day, I hope. (*Letters,* p. 254)

Regarding the purely geographical, social, and cultural details of the particular journey, Almqvist is extremely thorough. The means of communication were at the time of his youth and manhood mainly post-horses; in his old age he also made use of such exotic conveyances as railroad trains in France and river steamers on the Mississippi.

Almqvist's letters on his travels are detailed and comprehensive. Once could say that the writer consciously stores up impressions and bits of information. The letters contain raw material that in several instances he used later in his works of fiction. A well-known example is the introduction to "The Chapel" with its description of Värnanäs, which is outlined in a long letter to his wife sent from Ronneby on July 16, 1836. There are also passages in "Baron Julius K°" for which letters from his Östergötland and Västergötland journeys of 1827 and '29 are preliminary studies.

All this gives us insight into Almqvist's way of working, which will not be considered here in detail. But it is interesting to recall that on his journeys Almqvist often jotted down laconic comments on people and conditions in various localities he was passing through, and sometimes he sketched maps and made topographical notes.

Thus, the letters he sent his family on his travels were partly collections of material, and Almqvist was very anxious that the recipients take good care of them. As late as 1854 he wrote his family from America describing his travel letters in this way:

If, out of love for me, you keep all my letters—as I am sure you do—they may finally be made into an account of my travels, not intended for the public but for my dear ones; and quite a unique one. As the purpose of my letters has in the first place been the fulfillment of my dear duty to give you personally an account of my experiences from time to time and moreover to give you the pleasure of reading about this country and the people here, it is evident that the accounts of my journeys must be of quite a different kind from the ordinary "books of travels" that are published for the public. For my part my main purpose was to have you as much and as vividly as possible before my eyes and my mind, by talking to you about all sorts of things in my letters. The usual and orthodox books of travels aim at presenting political, geographical, and historical dissertations on the countries; I, on the other hand, am intent on informing you of the *impressions* that all the new things that I have seen and experienced, immediate, fresh, and vivid, have made on *me* and my imagination, as I have thought this would interest and amuse you more. Consequently, my letters should be called *impressions of travels* rather than descriptions of travels. From that, however, it does not follow that now and then when occasion arises, facts about local politics, language, geography, and history will not also appear. (*Letters,* p. 252)

Many of the letters from Almqvist's travels are in the nature of short stories; notable examples are the account of the visit to Lieutenant Colonel Gripenvald on June 9, 1827 (*Letters,* p. 73 f.), or the letter from America dated July 8, 1854, with its gloomy description of the burial of a child (*Letters,* p. 264). I would also draw attention to the tense adventure-filled atmosphere in his description of journeying through Värmland's forests, in his letter of January 22, 1824, and particularly the following well-drawn picture of the young blind woman at Hållsta posting-house singing the ballad of her tragic life. Almqvist writes from Gelsebo on July 7, 1829:

The most remarkable thing on the whole journey was, however, what happened at Hållsta. While we were waiting for horses, a blind girl appeared in the middle of the crowd of country people that usually gather at posting-houses. She was pale but had a round pleasant face and was very tidy. She at once went up to a fence and stood there with her hands folded and began to sing to us

and the whole gathering. The whole crowd of peasants fell silent
and listened, we too. She sang in a clear loud voice songs that she
had composed herself. There was particularly one song that was
pathetic in a charming way. It was a narrative of how she had gone
blind at the age of two while her mother was once out in the fields
carrying her in her arms. When she was six her father had been
drowned. At the age of eleven she had taken it into her head to
sing of such things as she perceived inward. It is true that there
was something mournful about the subjects but it was combined
with sublime happiness. It was strange to see how everybody around
her wept like children. She was not a stranger but lived in the
parish. She was now twenty-six, so that they had heard her many
times. Wrinkled old men and women, soldiers armed with axes
who had gathered to put out a forest fire, the coachman, and
travelers, all were moved, so that several of them quite forgot themselves; but the singer herself did not cry, her eyelids were closed
so that her face was not unlike a plaster cast; only her lips moved
and now and again there was a glimpse of very white teeth. She
stood quite still; but her voice and gestures sometimes seemed
almost smiling, which strengthened still more the impression of what
she was singing. (*Letters,* p. 85)

The same letter contains observations of quite another sort:

Now we went south to cross a moor where there was by the
roadside a gallows with a headless body on it. It was a man from
Wanäs who had thrown a child into the lake (you will remember,
Maria, reading about it in *Dagbladet*). He had been beheaded here
last spring and the parts of the body had been broken on the wheel
in the usual way, but recently to the great astonishment of the
neighborhood the head had come off the wheel. This was the talk
of Friabäck posting-house. People believed that somebody had stolen
the head in order to get the nail with which it had been attached.
This nail was supposed to be useful for many things, especially in
a harness, though I do not know how. (*Letters,* p. 87)

The Gelsebo letter is rich in material: the scene with the
blind singer looks as if it had been taken from one of Almqvist's
descriptions of country life, and the mystery of the headless
gallows-bird shows how harshly criminals were treated.

Almqvist's travel letters still have an unequaled freshness.
Their author is a gay and cheery observer, with a keen eye

for essentials of both the whole and the detail, and he presents his material in a captivating and at the same time objective manner. His style is expository, lucid, and simple (adapted to the recipients!) and his tone is the carefree manner of the uncommitted traveler on summer holidays, far from the worries of the workaday world. He clearly describes his pleasure in traveling in a letter from Kalmar dated July 11, 1836: apropos of the beautiful Fogelvik and its ailing owner, bowed beneath the weight of worries, he declares:

A traveling poet, on the contrary, can say without boasting that he owns everything that is beautiful in the whole country, for without being in the least troubled by the financial situation of all these places and the difficulties involved, there is nothing to prevent him from rejoicing and inhaling all the wonderful things that man and nature present everywhere. The owner himself hardly gets as much as that, for the cares of management make him suffer to such an extent that in the end he has to be taken care of himself. But at the first sign of trouble the poet leaves for another place; and so do the birds and so did I. (*Letters,* p. 105)

The image of the poet-traveler as an independent, carefree bird is a pertinent one, and Almqvist returns to it. In a letter to Atterbom of September 13, 1837, he reflects on the purpose and pleasure of traveling. He tries to acquire a wider knowledge of nature and humanity; he looks upon his travels as "the most real dramatic studies," and he sums up the result of the vicissitudes and hardships of traveling when he compares himself to a bird, sometimes picking away at a pile of wood-chippings, sometimes swinging on a honeysuckle branch.

CHAPTER 4

In the Yellow Parlor of the Hunting Seat

I *"The Hunting Seat" and Its Inhabitants*

IN "The Hunting Seat," subtitled "A Romantic Tale," we find a delight in nature and humanity similar to that which we noted in Almqvist's travel letters. Probably written in the late 1820s, "The Hunting Seat" was published in five books in 1833 (printing date: 1832) as volume I of *The Book of the Wild Rose* (duodecimo edition). In 1839, "The Hunting Seat" was reprinted in *The Book of the Wild Rose* (imperial octavo edition), this time with a sixth book, "The Man Who Hated God."

Thus, "The Hunting Seat" was printed as an introduction to both series of *The Book of the Wild Rose*, for this tale provides the framework for the whole collection of variegated genres and art forms encompassed in the splendidly structured work. It is explained in "The Hunting Seat" that the various parts of the *Wild Rose* work are told, sung, recited, or acted in the yellow parlor of the Närke hunting seat of the former Marshal of the Court, Herr Hugo Löwenstjerna. Every evening at six o'clock the persons acting as narrators and listeners gather around this nobleman.

The trick of using a fictional framework to compress various contributions from different persons is not in itself original. *The Arabian Nights, The Decameron, The Canterbury Tales,* and *Die Serapionsbrüder* are all familiar examples of this technique. But Almqvist has strung together not only short stories and anecdotes, but also works in other genres, including factual prose, and all the pieces fall into place like pearls. Even extremely disparate elements adapt to the external unity imposed by the frame technique. In a deeper sense, this idea of unity (which, incidentally, is intimately bound up with the dream of the *Gesamtkunstwerk*, to which I shall return) remained with Almqvist throughout his life. Works not included in *The Book of the Wild Rose* are often presented on the title pages as works by "the author of *The Book of the Wild Rose*," and in his old age, Almqvist was still dreaming of assembling all his manuscripts and published writings, even journalism and textbooks, in the *Wild Rose* frame.

In the third book of "The Hunting Seat"—to the accompaniment of bird cries, a mysterious flute melody, and rifle shots—the widely traveled and demonic farmer, Richard Furumo of Råbäcken, is introduced. He saves young Julianus Löwenstjerna's life and is made a member of the hunting seat academy where before long he comes to occupy the place of honor. Around Richard and Herr Hugo are grouped the latter's large family, including his children, Henrik, Frans, and Aurora; his brother, Andreas; his sister, Eleonora; his niece, Ulrika Sofia; and his nephew, Julianus. All these are active in the *Wild Rose* books, but Richard is the chief narrator. The two principal characters within the *Wild Rose* framework, Herr Hugo and Richard Furumo, are among those fictitious personages blessed with eternal life. They are both contrasting and complementary characters. To begin with, Herr Hugo is introduced by his interests and habits: he is a wealthy man of sixty, amiable and jovial.

In his youth he had been an excellent bibliophile and ardent reader, especially historical writing. He had a smattering of most civilized languages, and he had in his head a wider knowledge of antiquities than is to be found in most professors. He was also fond of literature, music, paintings; but above all, he followed events in the ancient as well as in the modern world, with an ardor that was perhaps somewhat moderated from the time of his adolescence onward when he held various posts in government service, but which now returned stronger than ever, as he sat in his armchair in his fairy tale manor-house. (*CW*, V, p. 13)

Herr Hugo, then, is aristocratic but at the same time democratic; he is somewhat verbose but well informed and interested.

He is genially critical, a little declamatory and self-satisfied, but infinitely obliging.

Richard Furumo, his foil and complement, is first introduced as an invisible flutist playing an inexpressibly beautiful tune, but shortly afterward he appears suddenly as a man of action; with a well-aimed shot, he kills a wolf that is about to kill Julianus. The young man looks at his rescuer,

[whose] tall but young, free, and easy form inspired confidence, showing that his home could not be bad, but that people could eat as well as drink there and have a merry evening together. He also looked at his clothes which were coarsely woven but none the worse for wear: they were well made according to their fashion, and durable; under his rough homespun jacket he particularly noted a waistcoat of a much finer quality. (*CW*, V, p. 47)

Richard has "big, grave eyes under black eyebrows; a nose not exactly large but straight; a mouth with full lips of an almost smiling shape," and "a rather low forehead under a rich head of hair" (*CW*, V, p. 56).

Unlike Herr Hugo, Richard Furumo is surprising and demonic, secretive and teasing. If one wants to compare him and Herr Hugo, one can apply E. M. Forster's division of characters into "flat" and "round."[1] The "flat" ones are, in their purest form, built up around a single idea or quality. They are viewed from one angle only, and they present no surprising features or qualities. The "round" characters are always viewed from more than one angle, they always have a new side to expose, and new qualities that surprise and deepen. If we apply this classification to Almqvist's figures, we find that Richard Furumo is a "round" character whereas Herr Hugo tends to be "flat."

Almqvist's contemporaries were inclined to identify *him* with Richard Furumo, and the author stated his opinion on this question on several occasions. As early as March 1834, he says (in a letter to Atterbom, with reference to a passage in the latter's review of "The Hunting Seat"): "It is not Richard Furumo through whom *I* speak—he is not my mask. Frans and Aunt Eleonora are as much that, in their way" (*Letters*, p. 91).

In a later letter to Atterbom (of January 27, 1839), he

complains about C. J. Lénström's otherwise very appreciative review in *Eos*. By applying the *"Erlebnisästhetik"* uncritically, Lénström had declared "that I am entirely worn out, which is bad enough." According to Almqvist, Lénström confused his own thoughts with

all that I have made several persons in my piece say, defend, and allege, which was, however, *only* from their points of view and a dramatic description of *them*. Now Lénström cannot bring together all *their* thoughts (which he believes to be mine) into *one* fundamental system, and that is why he regards me as worn out. Consequently, he declares quite categorically that Richard Furumo is the same person as Almqvist. He does not realize that it was my intention to represent Richard Furumo as a *demonic narrator* who, precisely because of his nature, has so many different elements to offer. If I myself were to be something in "The Hunting Seat," it would be the complex of Herr Hugo and Richard *together*: for in my person I have as much of the gay, happy, and talkative element (Herr Hugo's temperament) as of the demonic and somber element (Richard's temperament). (*Letters*, p. 137)

The function of "The Hunting Seat" as a frame story is most important. Here the *Wild Rose* work is introduced, the persons are brought in, and the narrative form and the meetings are motivated. But of course the story has a value of its own. The scene in which Julianus fights for his life against a wolf is related in a passage of pure suspense:

When Julianus had struck the wolf's forehead such a blow that one of its eyes hung down on the hairy cheek-bone, this was more than could be endured, and so, with a bold leap, the wolf sprang at Julianus's face, felled him down with his front paws, bared two rows of extremely sharp and beautiful white teeth close to Julianus's throat, and was with one bite about to dispatch Julianus's soul into the company of pale blue ghosts—when in the nick of time, there came a shot, a lead bullet tore into the wolf's throat and sent the wolf tumbling over twice toward the bank of the brook where it came to rest against a boulder with its belly upward. (*CW*, V, p. 45)

In an ironic, provoking, mysterious, and fragmentary way Richard Furumo talks of the beautiful sinner, Magdalena, and of her death. Julianus is shocked when from various quarters he learns that Richard Furumo was present at her death and that the girl was not killed in an accident. Eventually it becomes evident—though never explicitly stated—that Richard had tried to save Magdalena's soul by letting her die in a moment of contrition.

Of course, Richard's evasive, ironic way of telling the story in itself helps to characterize him and also his conception of death and life.

In "The Hunting Seat" Almqvist proves himself to be the perfect narrator from the very outset. In the first sentence he focuses on young Henrik Löwenstjerna, who comes singing through the forest where he has been hunting. Together with Henrik, the reader approaches the "Hunting Seat" from outside; the manor is "a white well-maintained building in noble style, long rather than high."

Seen from some distance, on its islet in the lake, it looked like a swan resting in peaceful grace, washed on all sides by transparent and cooling waves. Yet it was like the haughty beauty who lives alone, for herself only; for in the whole region no farmstead was to be seen, only dark stretches of pine forests along the shores of the lake lay before the eye, interrupted at intervals by ridges of gay, light-green birch trees, and in the far distance a wild, blue, vague mixture of clouds and trees merged into that immeasurable thing we are wont to call the vault of heaven. (*CW*, V, p. 8)

In Henrik's company the reader crosses the bridge to the manor islet, enters by the front door, goes up the stairs to the manor hall and finally enters the yellow parlor where the whole Löwenstjerna family are sitting: the clock has struck six—the hour for entertainment.

The scenery in "The Hunting Seat" is, as Henry Olsson points out, presented with remarkable intensity and a sense of what is artistically essential. He suggests that the mighty forests of Värmland have been combined with the pleasing Mälar setting to enhance Almqvist's superb descriptions.[2]

It is worthwhile analyzing the beginning of the third book of the *Wild Rose* for Almqvist's almost magical evocation of natural setting. He first appeals to the sense of hearing, then

to that of sight, and, at the end of the following passage, the
dying flute melody is compared to the flourish of color in the
leaves—genuine Romantic synaesthesia:

> A kind of hoarse and monotonous cry of waterfowl was now
> heard at a distance indicating that there was a lake up in the
> forest. At times sudden wing-beats of a hawk noisily broke through
> the air, and finally the cries of the woodcock completed the wild
> charm of this place. Then in the distance a shot was fired silencing
> all the birds. In the pure morning air the sound of the shot was
> repeated six times in all directions—more and more hollow according
> to the distance, more and more marvelous since no trace of the
> hunter himself who had fired the shot was to be seen or heard. [. . .]
> The cloudless sky was beautiful—the most pellucid and silent
> crystalline light was dozing in the firmament. Then slowly, slowly
> came the note of a flute.
> Then Julianus quickly raised his head. The tune played was simple
> enough and ran through everything like an invisible vein, but it
> had a haunting charm. [. . .] In his mind the music dissolved in vague
> floating beauty—like the trembling of the colors among the leaves
> early on a heavenly morning. (*CW*, V, p. 43 ff.)

The inhabitants of the "Hunting Seat" became popular and—
as has already been mentioned—Almqvist gave the frame story
a value of its own; it came to be referred to as "The Manor
House Chronicle." It narrated the experiences and adventures
of the Hunting Seat people and included not only "The Hunting
Seat" but also the novel, *Hinden* (*The Hind*), and the short
story, "Baron Julius K*."

II   *A Ghost Ballad*

The first parts of *The Book of the Wild Rose* were well received by the critics. Atterbom, the standard-bearer of Swedish
Romanticism wrote—by request—a long and appreciated review,
which concluded with a recommendation of this work, "a product
of passionate feeling, ingenious imagination, tragic experience
and *gay science*."[3]

In a letter of February 3, 1834, Almqvist commented on this
review and, encouraged by it, gave an account of the prospective
order within *The Book of the Wild Rose*. His list of finished

manuscripts and works already begun is of great value to scholars for the chronology it presents. This important letter is reprinted in *Letters* (pp. 89–92).

Another enthusiastic reader of Almqvist was the Finnish poet J. L. Runeberg whose assessment I shall consider later.

Between *The Hermitage* and *The Hind* Almqvist published the short ghost ballad "*Vargens dotter*" ("The Daughter of the Wolf"); its subtitle classifies it as a modern chiaroscura.

It is introduced in *The Book of the Wild Rose* when Richard Furumo gives a talk on ghosts, explaining why hardly any appear nowadays:

At the present time no living person loves another so inutterably that he returns to earth after death out of desire for company extending across the boundary of life. Nor has anyone such deep hatred of a person he knows that he wants to take the trouble to torment him after death. Add to this the extreme banality of our time, and I would like to know what soul would be interested in coming back to haunt people in a world in which he was bored so profoundly that death was undoubtedly a gain?—I predict that, if we were to enter on a more pleasant, youthful, and courageous period, if we had people who were greater in love and stronger in wrath, in short, if we had a more interesting earth to walk upon, then the ghosts would certainly come to us. (*CW*, V, p. 273)

But Richard Furumo presents a concrete example in the plot and background of the ballad to come:

On a journey in the neighborhood of Vingåker I heard about something that had happened there a decade or two earlier that filled everybody with dismay. Two young people were consumed with love, the girl's parents did not approve, the young persons found a way of escaping from the constraint; a poet, moved by what had happened, sang about it—what else do you want, Herr Hugo? (*CW*, V, p. 274)

Richard Furumo then presents an old tipstaff who, to the notes of a hurdy-gurdy, sings the ballad of poor Henrik and the rich farmer's daughter, Anna, who rather than submit to separation, commit suicide together. The lover's dead body is mutilated, but Henrik's ghost takes revenge.

The ballad strikes up with a brilliant, Ossian invocation:

> Singer, tune thy harp by the lake,
> Take the shining black bow in thy hand.
> I know thy strings are not of gold,
> Neither of silver, nor bronze, nor iron.
> But if thou hast strings of sinew, white and red,
> Spun of the fleeing stag's nerve,
> Then tune thy harp!
>
> (*CW*, V, p. 278)

There is an atmosphere of Romantic terror flavored with a sense of the popular chapbook about this ballad; it also indicates the range of Almqvist's register.

III The Hind

In 1833 Almqvist published not only "The Hunting Seat" but also *The Hermitage* (already discussed on p. 51) and *The Hind.* While *The Hermitage* is a historical novel in the spirit of Sir Walter Scott, *The Hind* is a topical novel of the day: like "The Hunting Seat," it might have been subtitled "A Romantic Tale of Our Own Time," but actually it is called "A Romaunt in Twelve Books." This designation, however, is preceded by "Scenes from the Chronicle of the 'Hunting Seat.'"

The Hind was probably written 1829–30 with certain later additions. Richard Furumo plays no part, either as character or narrator; the chief narrators are Uncle Andreas and Aunt Eleonora. The seventh book contains diary notes and memoirs of the unfortunate Andreas Löwenstjerna, presenting intimate psychological studies of the recently deceased man. The diary and letter form derives from the sentimental novel of the eighteenth century, but is also not far removed from drama. Almqvist uses the epistolary form in a masterly fashion; I need only mention the excellent short story written in letters, "Araminta May," and the first book of *The Queen's Jewel.*

The main subject of *The Hind* is marriage and family life; several scholars believe that the author's own experiences and fragile marriage are an important source.

The Hind offers further details on the origin of the Hunting

Seat chronicle manuscript: Herr Hugo has ordered a few "editors" to take down the "largely improvised" tales,

because he considered that nothing was properly preserved and insured against loss if it was not kept within the covers of a bound book. He even decided that besides the evening tales, everything that happened inside and outside the manor to the members of the family or the people living in the neighborhood should be recorded in a special volume so as to form a *manor house chronicle*.

It is under these circumstances that the transcription has commenced, and the work has expanded, grown and is still growing. It is not possible to know when it will end. (*CW*, V, p. 466 f.)

Consequently, we can add to the manuscript and publisher fictions an "editor" fiction, the purpose of which is to heighten the credibility of the Hunting Seat, its inhabitants, and its tales.

And a little later appears the Romantics' dream of a *Gesamtkunstwerk* embodied in manuscript form:

"What is your opinion," said Frans. "My father intends to make a composition of music, paintings, and all our tales, in prose as well as verse, so as to form one great artistic whole which, however, must live only as a manuscript." (*CW*, V, p. 488 f.)

Finally, in *The Hind*, the title, *The Book of the Wild Rose*, is explained in a passage showing Herr Hugo finding a broken-off wild rose in the woods, taking it home, and "laying it on top of his whole collection of tales and stories" (*CW*, V, p. 473). It is intended to imbue all Herr Hugo's papers with its fragrance.

IV   "Songes"

Novelist Fredrika Bremer was no friend of Almqvist, but in 1842, when she had listened to a few of his "*Songes*," she wrote the following to a friend:

Almqvist understands heaven; he has been there himself and there he has heard—not what he has given us in novels and philosophisms—but what he says in tones, in music. He has heard the heavenly choirs. He has noted them down. What a pity that I should not have heard them before today.[4]

As early as the 1820s we hear similarly enthusiastic opinions from Malla Silfverstolpe, Atterbom, and others. And one modern scholar has suggested that perhaps Almqvist made his most original literary contribution with "*Songes*," "whose poetic and, not least, musical novelty seems to have had the effect of a revelation upon his contemporaries."[5]

Most of Almqvist's lyric poetry is spontaneous and direct. It consists chiefly of short verses which he set to music. Fifty of his seventy to eighty musical poems were published under the title "*Songes*" (= Dreams) in the imperial octavo edition of *The Book of the Wild Rose* II (1849). The majority of them, however, date from the 1820s and '30s; Almqvist talks about their origins in a letter to Vendela Hebbe on July 17, 1843:

People usually imagine that, in order to compose charming poetry or music, one must have beautiful, peaceful, sweet surroundings to inspire or sustain one's imagination. This, however, is quite the contrary of what I have experienced.

If you turn to page 102 of the imperial octavo edition, you will find, under "Awakening," a very short poem beginning: "Listen to the clear, murmuring, slow whispering of the spring!" This is the first of all the pieces printed here. It was born to me in the middle of an indescribably rainy, dirty, autumn day while I was in a pretty melancholy mood, walking along some of the ugliest streets in Stockholm. It's always when things around me are at their most disgusting that the innermost images of my soul and their tones flash in my mind. At that point I had no instrument and hardly a regular home. I went to see one of my friends, the owner of a wreck of an old out-of-tune piano. At that keyboard I wrote down the music to "Listen to ... the spring" on a slip of paper, put it in my pocket, and left.

All the most beautiful songs were conceived in much the same way. "Solaviv's Song" came over me on my way from the city to Carlberg where at that time I used to go to teach the cadets. I then lived in a very shabby little room in Professor Ågren's house. At that time, I was discharging his extremely boring and laborious teaching program at Carlberg (in geography, the Swedish language, English, composition, and God knows what else). When I got up to my little room, I set Solaviv to music, without an instrument, since there wasn't any.

The piece No. 1 of the *"Songes"* ("Oh God, how beautiful ...") came to me in Östergötland at a place called Påtorp where the

68 CARL JONAS LOVE ALMQVIST

surroundings were fairly pleasant, "The Song of the Moon" at another place in Östergötland, near Lake Roxen, where I spent some time.— Several melodies (e.g., "Why did you come to the meadow?" No. 24 of the *"Songes,"* and others) came to me in a carriage or a coach, but the majority in Stockholm under the most painful circumstances while I was planning and organizing Nya Elementarskolan, writing my Arithmetic, the Orthography, and Geometry, having continual meetings with Hartmansdorff and refreshing myself in between with music. (*Letters,* p. 175 f.)

On the outside of the letter the recipient has written "extremely interesting," and she was right.

The *"Songes"* have an exquisitely simple naïve style and are in glaring contrast to the contemporary rhetorical poetry produced by Tegnér or Stagnelius. On the other hand, they are reminiscent of Geijer's lyric songs and Runeberg's *Idyls and Epigrams.* From a musical point of view, Almqvist's *"Songes"* also have traits in common with Geijer and the folk song.

The themes of the *songes* are fundamental ones: love and death, God and resurrection. The subjects vary from nordic, as in *"Sång till människooffret i det stora Blothuset i Sigtuna"* ("Song at the Human Sacrifice in the Great Temple in Sigtuna"), to exotic, as in *"Maïnours sång vid Eufrat"* ("Maïnour's Song on the Euphrates").

The combining of text and music tends to break up the stanza and meter; this further accents the deliberately simple and naïve, sometimes poetically rugged form.

In terms of motif and subject matter, the *songes* can be grouped as *nature* lyrics, for instance, *"Uppvaknandet"* ("Awakening")— mentioned by Almqvist in his letter to Vendela Hebbe—*religious* songs such as *"Solavivs sång"* ("Solaviv's Song"), and others on subjects taken from *Murnis* but also poems of a more Moravian character, as *"Den lyssnande Maria"* ("Listening Mary") or *"Hjärtats blomma"* ("The Flower of the Heart").

In addition there are *exotic songes* such as "Maïnour's Song on the Euphrates" or "Jem," and finally *realistic* poems like *"Fiskarsång vid Kalmar"* ("The Fisherman's Song at Kalmar"), *"Varför kom du på ängen?"* ("Why Did You Come to the Meadow?") with its rustic fiddle tones and the folk song or the gay, defiant, and brilliant *"Världens slut"* ("End of the World").

There is also the short but concise *songe* called "*Marias häpnad*" ("Mary's Amazement"):

> White lambs are grazing in the meadow;
> But the child Jesus is also there.
>
> Mary stops amazed and calls:
> "I see a halo round his hair!" (*CW*, XIV, p. 55)

An instant of happiness and vision is captured; one sees only "a glimpse of white on green and then the halo, but the whole scene is rendered with the clarity and the naïve expressiveness of illuminated medieval manuscripts."[6]

"*Du går icke ensam*" ("You Are Not Alone") is a metaphysical *songe* about man and the stars:

> If, out of a thousand stars,
> Just one is looking at you,
> Believe in the meaning of that star,
> Believe in the radiance of her eye.
> You are not alone.
> The star has a thousand friends;
> All are watching you,
> Watching for her sake,
> You are happy and blessed.
> Heaven will have you tonight.
> (*CW*, XIV, p. 88)

This *songe* refers to a man who feels like a stranger on earth and sings of the liberation that man wins at the moment of death.[7]

There is also the beautiful *songe* about the mystic who was allowed to look into the home of the heart and afterward remained a guest and a stranger on this earth of ours. It is "*Antonii sång*" ("Antonius's Song"):

> With delight I looked into the house of the heart, listening:
> White figures approached me, answered, beckoning to me.
> Amazed I saw the eternal lands of sunshine:
> From the shores of the blessed, tones stole up to me.
> After that I never found delight in the world.
> After that I never, never found delight in the world.
> (*CW*, XIV, p. 30 f.)

The frightening, almost brutal *"Häxan i konung Karls tid"* ("The Witch in King Charles's Time") stands on its own:

> Here on the top of the hill lie the old woman's black bones:
> She who burned last spring at the stake.
> Now you shall hear the tale of the red fire:
> Hear how the old woman was put on the pyre to burn.
> The woman had taken sticks of white pine.
> But she stuck her sticks into a wall.
> Slowly she went up to the wall and from the sticks
> She milked with trembling hands for her little children.
> But the sweet milk came from the rich parson's cow.—
> The children saw their mother burned to death.
>
> (*CW*, XIV, p. 52)

"The Witch in King Charles's Time" has been praised as a masterpiece, and rightly so. It is an early *songe* from the period around 1830, 1833 at the latest. It presents a realistic scene in highly concrete detail, beginning with the words of coloration, calling up visions of sparking red fire and black charred death. Almqvist poses the poor woman and her little children as a contrast to the rich parson; the poet's social and religious radicalism is anticipated.

Before the clinching final line of the poem comes a dash pregnant with meaning; here Almqvist lets the reader supply the sequence of events. The parson reports her, she is interrogated and condemned: in place of all this stands a dash. Through the omission and the pause, the final line makes a greater impact, heightened still further by the horror of the matter and the detached matter-of-factness of the tone.

This *songe* is in accord with the aesthetics propounded in the "Dialogue on How to Finish Pieces," but at the same time, like the other *songes*, it is characterized by the stylistic ideal of naïveté: it tries to convey the impression of spontaneity and artlessness through deliberately clumsy formulations, banal particles, frequent repetitions, a simple paratactic construction, etc. This naïve stylistic ideal has in this poem been combined with a tendency toward concreteness or realism, and the result is an excellent example of what Almqvist calls "poetry of facts," the special poetry of things and events.

As the poem was written around 1830, its pronounced sense of social concern is remarkable. Ten years later it would have been less notable. By then Almqvist had committed himself to a course of social agitation: it was then quite natural for him to write poems with a social message. But around 1830 Almqvist was absorbed in religio-mystic quietism, aloof from the world. Obviously, the motif affected him so deeply that it pierced the armor of quietism and created a poem full of social sympathy and indignation.

Forest mysticism and longing for death are combined in the suggestive piece *Björninnan* ("The Bear") which might almost be called a tale with an inlaid *songe*; however, "The Bear" is an independent part of the first volume of *The Book of the Wild Rose* (the imperial octavo edition). The tale relates how the young peasant boy, Erik, who is hunting a female bear accidentally shoots and kills his beloved. From the forest Erik then hears a strange, wonderful song. Death seems to call him until he finds the bear, wrestles with her, and dies. The first stanza of the mysterious song is as follows:

> Come into the wood, fair boy, come, oh come!
> Here is the lovely
> Garden of death:
> From here the spirit of your beloved
> Rose to the beautiful heaven of bright stars.
> Do you remember,
> Oh, do you remember
> My breast when you fired?
> Come into the wood, my boy, come, oh come!
> Here are roses,
> Kisses, and death.
> Remember the color of my eyes, oh come!
>   (*CW*, XIII, p. 178)

The distinguished poet Zacharias Topelius has testified to the Almqvist fever that spread through Finland in the 1830s and '40s:

He fell as it were from the moon. The first impression was wonder, the second questioning uncertainty, the third admiration, which among the majority of young people soon grew into enthusiasm. Never had people read anything like that. The boldness and originality of the style, the mysterious poetry of the substance where the most airy Romanticism alternated with playful, at times scathing satire, it was all enchanting, like a dream. People forgot to criticize, they were carried away, unable to resist this dazzling, floating wave of "roses, kisses, and death." As "Come into the Wood" was sung or "Arthur's Hunt" was recited, no poetry had ever been recited in Finland before.[8]

V *The* Gesamtkunstwerk

As Fredrik Böök has pointed out, we often find the aesthetic theory of the "Dialogue on How to Finish Pieces" demonstrated in "*Songes.*" Almqvist does not give "a complete picture or a conclusive, transparent state of mind," says Böök,

he stirs the imagination by a mysterious touch, he arouses, by an inexplicable image, a strange man, wondering or curiosity that are not satisfied; in that very chiaroscuro, in the uncertain and floating, unsuspecting state of mind into which one is brought, a fleeting and elusive but intense emotional response is aroused. It is the most radical Romantic poetry that we possess in Swedish.[9]

Regarding Almqvist's qualities as musician, most experts— contemporary as well as more recent—are agreed in calling atten- tion to both the dilettantism of his compositions and the in- genious improvisation that characterizes them. This applies equally to his eleven books of piano pieces *Fria fantasier för piano-forte* (*Improvisations for the pianoforte*) which began to appear in 1847. His aversion to excessive conformity to the laws of musical theory is also evident in his essays "On the Unity of Epic and Drama" and "*Om musikens framtid*" ("On the Future of Music"), the latter of which was later incorporated in "On the Poetry of Facts."

In uniting words and music, "*Songes*" expresses the Romantic ambition welding together different genres and art forms, but in the prose introduction to "*Songes,*" Almqvist provides them with a further dimension. He clearly regards them as little stage plays, *tableaux vivants,* full of movement and sound. He has Herr Hugo's sons give detailed directions:

For each piece a single, brief, and finished, easily comprehensible and plastically beautiful situation is chosen (if of course we have anything beautiful at hand). The theater—as such we use the yellow parlor, particularly suited for this purpose on account of its length—is arranged by hanging across the middle of the room a curtain of white gauze, which divides the whole room into two equal parts, one part in front of the gauze and one behind it. This curtain is *never* raised. We spectators sit on one side of the gauze. On the other side, at the extreme back of the stage, the dream takes place. [. . .]

The dreamlike performances that my father intends to arrange are of course in the nature of short stage plays [. . .] each one simply aims to be an individual performance in its own right possessing a significance of its own and no other; but always musical in character as well as plastic and drastic. (*CW*, XIV, p. 12)

Thus, the *songes* are intended to be staged; the gauze gives a sophisticated touch of vagueness to the persons and their activity. Words, music, color, action: everything unites in these little works of art. They provide an important variant of the Romantics' dream of the *Gesamtkunstwerk*.

In the same way—as we have already seen—Almqvist, in *The Hind*, has Herr Hugo present his great idea of a work of art consisting of painting, music, and poetry in the same mould, where the image and the music are not supplementary illustrations of the poem, not "a superfluous decoration but a necessary integral part of the whole and, what is more, in an organic way" (*CW*, V, p. 486 f.). As time went on, this harmony of the arts that the Romantics and Almqvist recommended was again brought to the fore by the Symbolists and by Wagner's musical drama.

But it is also important to point out the interest in the fragment, the aesthetics of the incomplete. Almqvist himself declared that the "Dialogue on How to Finish Pieces" refers to nearly all parts of *The Book of the Wild Rose*. And an expert sums up:

The more or less disharmonious form of these poems finds another explanation here. The sporadic, the isolated, and the tentative stand out as the result not only of a linguistic effort or musical influence but also of intellectual deliberation. The flexible form is meant to reflect a sense of the infinity of the subject, of any subject. Thus, in many respects the *songes* will exemplify their creators opinion of art—aesthetics of inspiration which were in reality aesthetics of experiment.[10]

CHAPTER 5

The Queen's Jewel

I Origin, Motifs, Characters

IN a letter to Atterbom dated May 9, 1834, Almqvist wrote
that he had finished "a composition which has greatly interested me and which I brought to a close the other day with a
certain sense of bliss" (*Letters*, p. 93). It was *The Queen's
Jewel*, which was published in November of the same year.
The book was then sent to Atterbom with a letter in which
the author stressed the novel's elaborate construction.

I venture to assert that, as regards inner architecture, it is artistically
composed. As for the execution, I think you will find it lively; I have
attached great importance to the invention of the actual situation
and what the situation shows is the essential thing. It is true that
everything is dressed in a historical costume but as regards the
historical personages concerned, I have not demanded of them
anything which was not in keeping with their well-known historical
character: moreover, people will soon see that a higher idea runs
through the whole work. (*Letters*, p. 94 f.)

The Queen's Jewel was published as the fourth part of *The
Book of the Wild Rose,* and its complete title reads as follows:
*The Queen's Jewel or Azouras Lazuli Tintomara. A Tale of
What Happened Immediately Before, During, and After the
Assassination of Gustav III.* It is provided with an introduction
and a conclusion that attaches it to the *Wild Rose* frame, where,
according to the fiction, it is read aloud in the yellow parlor
of the Hunting Seat. In the introduction, the editor and narrator, Richard Furumo, gives an account of his meeting with
the surviving principal characters and finally takes out "a little
parcel wrapped up in soft East India straw-paper" (*CW*, VI,

75

p. 12). And after producing this concrete manuscript evidence, he begins what is properly the narrative of the conspiracy leading to the assassination of Gustav III on March 16, 1792, and the subsequent Reuterholm government.

To sum up the plot: In connection with the assassination of the King, the beautiful hermaphrodite Tintomara is involved in an important and confused sequence of events in which —involuntarily—she is to spread misery and death around her until she herself is killed. The series of events has a political and an erotic aspect.

As far as politics are concerned, Tintomara acts as the tool of the conspirators in two ways. She steals the Queen's jewel, which—without her knowledge—is disposed of to get money for the change of regime; and she also unintentionally entices the King into staying on at the masked ball, which culminates in his death.

At the same time Tintomara becomes the center of an erotic adventure.

Two officers, Captain Ferdinand and Major Clas Henrik, who are involved in the conspiracy, are in love with the sisters Amanda and Adolfine M. Owing to a misunderstanding, jealousy arises, not only between the sisters but also between their admirers. The idyl, reestablished only with difficulty, is wrecked on the night of the assassination because Amanda believes that the King, who is pursuing Tintomara, is Ferdinand pursuing Adolfine and that Ankarström, who shoots the King, is Clas Henrik. After an exciting flight upstairs behind the wings, Adolfine first meets Tintomara and then watches the famous ballet pantomime which is a résumé of all that happens in the novel, and then she takes a nocturnal walk in the streets of Stockholm in company with Ankarström, the assassin of the King—a scene which is one of the highlights of the book.

After the assassination, Tintomara again divides the couples. Down in Kolmården Ferdinand and Clas Henrik fall in love with Tintomara, and so do Amanda and Adolfine, believing that she is (may be) a man. Tintomara, however, extricates herself and is brought back to Stockholm by Reuterholm, who wants to exploit her for further political machinations. The two sisters go mad; Ferdinand kills Clas Henrik.

Tintomara escapes from Reuterholm but after various adventures she is caught and sentenced to death. A theatrical fake execution, complete with blank cartridges, is prepared, but standing in the firing squad, Ferdinand has loaded his rifle with live ammunition, and he shoots a bullet through her heart.

The most important motifs of the novel are above all the qui pro quos of the masked ball, the hermaphrodite motif, the motif of illegitimate birth, the motif of elective affinity, the motif of the noble savage, the animal vs. man contrast, the heathen vs. Christian contrast. They are brilliantly projected in the antithetical motto of the whole work: "Tintomara! Two things are white: Innocence and Arsenic."

Tintomara is a seventeen-year-old dancer at the opera, the illegitimate daughter of the actress Clara and of Baron Munck and consequently the half sister of Gustav IV Adolf, who is thirteen at the time of the action. Tintomara has not been baptized but has been named after some twenty plays or ballets. She is androgynous, i.e. of both male and female sex, though as one of the surgeons in the novel comments: "I do not know whether the term androgynous ought to apply to a person of neither sex or one of both sexes" (*CW*, VI, p. 68).

The Tintomara figure has become one of Almqvist's most fascinating creations. She is attractive, baffling, evasive, and finally as unapproachable as the genius of Almqvist's poetry. She embodies a multitude of contrasts. She is both man and woman (or neither man nor woman); she is heathen and Christian; she is an animal and human being; she is conscious reason and blind nature; she belongs to both earth and heaven. She is—in Almqvist's own terminology, borrowed from Neo-Platonism—an "animal coeleste," a "celestial animal." Tintomara embodies the union of spirit and nature and also aesthetic playfulness: free, beautiful, irresponsible and capricious as the fanciful twists of an arabesque. Schelling and Schiller are her godfathers.

In Tintomara's temperament, however, there is something of Almqvist's seemingly indifferent attitude toward human commitment and passion. A personal note is perceptible when Tintomara pours out her despair at seeming cold in the face of other people's misery. "You are lying, you are lying. I am no tiger" (*CW*, VI, p. 268).[1]

Tintomara and Amorina have traits in common; they are both alone, both have great power over people but are outcasts of society, foredoomed to be imprisoned as malefactors or else perish. Both are attractive and genuinely innocent, and both are promised a better life after death.

Scholars have also found literary models for various aspects of Tintomara's personality: among her literary cousins they have noted particularly Goethe's Mignon, Sir Walter Scott's Fenella (in *Peveril of the Peak*), and also the little gypsy girl Esmeralda in Victor Hugo's novel *Notre Dame de Paris*.[2]

Most of the novel is set in Stockholm and its environs, the district of Kolmården and the bay of Bråviken. The whole range of the social spectrum is covered from court and aristocratic circles to the barracks of the White Guards, a prison, the usurer Cohen's house, and Tintomara's poor home where she lived with her destitute mother, Clara. Just as the cathedral dominates Victor Hugo's *Notre Dame de Paris*, Gustav III's Opera House dominates *The Queen's Jewel*.

The setting of Almqvist's novel is conjured up in a masterly fashion; the Opera House, with its fantastic mixture of light and shadow, affords a striking illumination for the masque. It has been noted that, in his famous poem celebrating the fiftieth anniversary of the Swedish Academy, Tegnér viewed the period of Gustav III in a bright, sunny light whereas Almqvist had been charmed by its twilight; chiaroscuro, he believed, was the appropriate light of the period. By and large, it is a glittering and baffling world of masque and theater that prevails in the novel. Even the final scene, with the execution of Tintomara, becomes highly theatrical and unreal. But at the same time the theatrical setting is counterbalanced effectively by the beautiful summer scenery of Kolmården in the latter part of the novel: the landscape behind Tintomara's famous song is the actual forest, not stage scenery.

We find excellent portraits of young women in the characters of the two sisters, Amanda and Adolfine. There is the tense description of Adolfine's confused and frightened escape through the wings of the Opera House immediately after the King has been assassinated. High up in the attic's labyrinths the feverish, desperate young woman meets Tintomara, who helps her to escape from her pursuers. Running, Adolfine glimpses the rehearsal of a ballet pantomime, which incidentally functions artistically as a reflected image of the action of the whole novel, "a play within the play." (I shall refer later in greater detail to this important method of composition.)

Adolfine's flight then continues out of the Opera House onto the streets of Stockholm. Here she meets a masked stranger who subsequently turns out to be Ankarström, the murderer of the King. The young woman's confusion and fear are increased by the murderer's strange, macabre, masochistic conversation. By means of half-suppressed comments and hints, the atmosphere—charged from the outset—sustains an almost insupportable tension at the lonely Packartorget where executions take place. These are the concluding lines of the scene between Ankarström and Adolfine. He wants to familiarize himself with the fate that is awaiting him at this place of execution, and so he asks Adolfine:

then do what I am asking you to do, which is also only a game—my head is now resting on your knee—I am making myself familiar with your knee—I think of it as my block, my last pillow. Don't take it amiss if I hold on to you with both my arms, for if I didn't you would run away from me, I can tell that by your nervous twitchings. But I don't want you to—stay here—and don't tremble—you be my block! Now, now—my neck is bare!—Pass a finger across my neck. I want to get to know the feeling of it. Be my executioner. I want to make myself familiar with my last acquaintance. All your limbs are aquiver! Can you not be my executioner just for fun! There's nothing to it! Do as I tell you! Do as I order you!! Obey!!! Stretch out your middle finger, and pass it across my neck. Fainting? Well, shut your eyes, girl, I don't mind; but pass your finger across my neck! (*CW*, VI, p. 123 f.)

The scene is written with profound psychological insight, and in the figure of Ankarström, we find a further instance of Almqvist's interest in criminals and their treatment.

II *Epic and Dramatic Elements*

In narrative technique *The Queen's Jewel* is strongly reminiscent of *Amorina*; both works alternate epic and dramatic form
although the epic claims a higher proportion in *The Queen's
Jewel*: a word-count shows three tenths of the text to be epic
narration and seven tenths direct speech (monologue, dramatic,
and epic dialogue). On one occasion Almqvist himself under-
lined the similarity of the two works; on another he called *The
Queen's Jewel* a fugue bearing "a family likeness to *Amorina*":
but it was, he thought, "better than *Amorina*" (*CW*, VI, p. vii).

Almqvist supplies further justification for this alternation of
epic and dramatic form in the novel itself. In several instances
he has Richard Furumo (who functions as a sort of cross
between editor and fictitious author) remark upon narrative
technique, bringing us into the author's workshop. That which in
Amorina was a play with illusion or broken illusion, becomes
here a matter of verification of the sequence of events—inasmuch
as the author's activity is part of the fiction of the novel in
quite a different way. The fictitious author presents, or instance,
his fictitious sources:

"They consist of information given to me by my hospitable
hosts at Ribbingsholm, partly by word of mouth, partly on paper,
in the form of letters, court proceedings, scenes and conversations
recorded then and there. The result has been that my account
must perforce be somewhat fragmentary and often consist of
casual scenes; *pass from epic into drama and then back again*"
(*CW*, VI, p. 158 f.; my italics). I should also draw attention
to what Richard Furumo says in the introduction (*CW*,
VI, p. 11 f.).

As to the epic elements, one thing the narrator does is to
deliver exclamatory addresses to the listening Herr Hugo and
his circle. This apostrophizing goes on from the first pages
of the novel to the last. At times they are open appeals to the
imagination: "I ask you, Herr Hugo, to imagine the Stockholm
Opera House auditorium [. . .] You will please direct your special
attention to two wings" (*CW*, VI, p. 74). But the narrator also
addresses the characters that he is just describing: "Charming

nun! Why should you come here on this black evening!" (*CW*, VI, p. 87, cf p. 101).

This method implies that the narrator has an audience to speak to, a Herr Hugo to represent all other readers as listeners. It is—as has already been pointed out—justified by the *Wild Rose* frame. How does this normally work? The opening of the third book serves as an example of Almqvist's jovial manner of *beginning* pieces; it also demonstrates his talent for creating a retarding state of suspense in both the reader and the character.

In her room Adolfine, like the reader, is excitedly awaiting news of the outcome of the duel between the admirers of her sister and herself. "At this moment Fritz, the footman, came in from the entrance hall by the other door of the cabinet. 'Hurry up, hurry up!' Miss Adolfine called to him in a low but eager voice [. . .] 'Hurry up! Tell me all about it, everything, accurately and quickly.'

'Dear Miss Adolfine . . .' Fritz began his account. But it is impossible to refrain from saying a few words first about the character of a footman who is very important for the story. He had been a faithful retainer of the W. family for so long [. . .]" (*CW*, VI, p. 48 f.). Here we see the narrator intervene, making a circumstantial digression for the benefit of the reader and presenting a detailed testimonial of the footman's service. When these (to say the least) irrelevant details—running more than a page—are disposed of and Fritz gets a word in at last, he follows the same procedure with Adolfine. The loquacious footman continually sidetracks with irrelevant information, and it is not till nine pages later that Adolfine—and the reader—manage to elicit from him the fact that, in the end, the duel never took place.

This style of narrating, comic and at the same time compelling, was quite common in Pre-Romantic and Romantic novels. Diderot and Sterne practiced the device, and so did Jean Paul and the German Romantics. Almqvist, however, used it sparingly but effectively.

A contrast to this narrative technique appears in the introduction to Book IX with its objective, straightforward, lucid account of the scenery around Bråviken and Kolmården, a piece of actual geographical description of the highest order.

Of the twelve books of the novel, Books II, III, V, and parts of VI, XI, and XII are narrated in the accepted sense of the word. The whole of Book I is in the form of correspondence, which is, as already stated, a form of narrative akin to dramatic dialogue.

Thus the exposition of *The Queen's Jewel* is provided by the principal figures of the novel themselves in the initial correspondence. And the novel concludes with Richard Furumo quoting fragments from yet another letter containing an eyewitness account of the circumstances surrounding Tintomara's death.

From Book VII on, the books are divided into scenes, a designation also used for the purely epic settings, as for instance IX:6 or XI:2. In IX:6 Furumo explicitly warns: "Here the scene is not dramatic; there is no speech" (*CW*, VI, p. 217).

The alternation of epic and dramatic form is motivated in *The Queen's Jewel* by the fictitious editor's remarks (see above p. 80) which are meant to give an illusion of authenticity to the quoted letters and the recorded conversations. Thus we can say that the dramatic elements of the novel are "real" while the omniscient narrator's epic narrative and comment are, according to the same fiction, the editor's explanations and additions, statements based on oral information given by persons involved in the novel.

As in *Amorina*, the dialogue sections are brilliant, vivid, and character-revealing: it is no mere chance that the stage adoptions of these novels met with great success in the 1950s and 1960s.

III *The Structure of the Novel*

We have already quoted a letter (see p. 75 above) in which Almqvist stressed the elaborate construction of his work and pointed out that its inner architecture was "artistically composed." This artistry shows itself in several ways in the composition: essential elements of the action following the assassination of the King are anticipated in a summing-up scene: namely, the ballet pantomime in Book VI. One of those present, the gentleman with the snuffbox, illustrates the pattern of this pantomime by holding up a five of spades, corresponding to Tintomara dressed in black in the middle, surrounded by two young men and two women, also dressed in black. From this moment on playing cards and their pattern take on a significant role. The symbolism of playing cards of various suits and values shows how Tintomara attracts the characters she meets. The pattern of the ballet pantomime reappears in concrete form in the farewell scene at Lindamot and at the end when the theatrical execution in Solna forest suddenly becomes serious.

Thus, the unity of the work is emphasized by the concrete image of the fable, but further parallels and omens frequently contribute to the balance and artistry of the composition.

The purpose of the ballet master's plan for the pantomime, explained by the gentleman with the snuffbox, is for the female savage, Tintomara, to charm the pantomime chief and become "the serene sovereign of her own master" (*CW*, VI, p. 108). In Book XI, Reuterholm has the same plan with regard to Duke Karl and Tintomara. Tintomara notices the parallel herself and compares Reuterholm to a dancing master; she says that in all pantomimes, she herself has "only been accustomed to carrying out the plan that some dancing master has given me" (*CW*, VI, p. 292). In both cases the plans are thwarted by Tintomara backing out of the pre-arranged pattern and escaping from the chief of the savages and Duke Karl, respectively (*CW*, VI, p. 323).

Clas Henrik and Ferdinand become enemies on account of a woman (in Book I) and face each other with weapons in their hands in the duel that was never fought (Book III); this finds a parallel in the rivalry for Tintomara and the enmity in Books X and XI, which lead to Ferdinand's assassination of Clas Henrik. Ankarström's murder of the King also corresponds to Ferdinand's assassination of Tintomara. The execution of Tintomara is followed by the execution of Ferdinand. The shooting practice with playing cards as the targets presages the sham execution. Thus, parallels and varied repetitions are common, constituting an important element of the work.

Even in this respect the musical fugue can be said to be the model. As has been mentioned several times, "the poetical fugue" represents for the author a synthesis of epic and dramatic form. In the case of Almqvist, who is musical and artistic, we cannot, however, dismiss the possibility that the strict scheme of composition of the musical fugue—with repetitions and

variations of a given theme, mirror effects, etc.—may have served
as a model for his variation of motifs, as in *The Queen's Jewel*.[3]
A statement by Almqvist in a letter to Atterbom of January 1,
1839 (*Letters*, p. 137 f.) concerning "The Palace" and *Godolphin*
"whose connection is that of a fugue" may also support such
an interpretation. It must, however, be stressed that these two
different interpretations of "fugue" are not contradictory but
complementary to each other.

IV   *Aesthetic Theory and Biographical Background*

Certain critics considered the ending of *The Queen's Jewel*
vague and immature—incidentally, a criticism leveled against
several other of Almqvist's works of that period. In self-defense,
Almqvist wrote his "Dialogue on How to Finish Pieces." There
are, he says here, two ways of writing. One is to supply complete
information. The reader need only read and accept. This is
the direct method, whereby nothing is omitted; the work exists
independently of the reader; it is integrated, completed, finished.

The other approach is not to say everything. Then the reader
carries on, joins in the creation of the work, "he does not only
read poetry, he becomes poetry" (*CW*, VII, p. 213). Here we
find the technique of the touch that awakens the world and
the reader; the fraction, the fragment becomes the aesthetic
pattern, for "the right fragment, like life, is more artistic in its
broken state than if it were whole" (*CW*, VII, p. 215).

Here Almqvist formulates his version of current Romantic
theories, as he practiced them in *Amorina* (cf. above p. 41),
in "*Songes*," in *Ramido Marinesco*, and in *Sviavígamál*. The
German Romantics, notably the Schlegels in their journal,
Athenäum, attach great value to the fragment. At the same
time, as has already been suggested, all this presages modern
demands for an engagé and participatory reader.

For the moment I shall deal only with what Almqvist says in
"Dialogue on How to Finish Pieces" about the ending of the
novel and about Tintomara's character. He has Richard Furumo
give his own interpretation of Tintomara's end:

I cannot remember that during the conception of this final scene
I was aware of any other intention or mood than the pleasure of

seeing Solna forest around me in my imagination. I also felt overjoyed at the thought of Azouras now being allowed to die. (*CW*, VII, p. 215 f.)

The conception of death expressed here coincides with that presented in *Murnis*, "*Songes*," etc.; it is also interesting to draw a comparison with the Magdalena episode in "The Hunting Seat": in both cases the chief concern is to save a person for death at a moment when she is in a state of grace.

Herr Hugo speaks and incidentally supplies a rapid characterization of the people in the group to which both Tintomara and the seemingly cool Richard Furumo belong:

I have known persons who at times, when emotion runs high in their hearts, fall silent because of its excess or, if their mouths speak, can only find works for trifling matters, perhaps just jokes. However, I am not so completely blind that I regard such a thing as *infernal iciness*, since I am well enough acquainted with the human mind to know that the most heartfelt and wonderful warmth sometimes expresses itself precisely in this way. The mysteries of life and heart often manifest themselves as contradictions. (*CW*, VII, p. 220)

At the same time this is a characterization of Almqvist himself and an extremely important one; it is interesting to follow his observations on this strange lack of feeling that seems to be such a fundamental feature of his character, which could also be extremely warm and enthusiastic. Almqvist must have been aware of this duality in his emotional life and understood its impact on the world around him, for he was very frequently at pains to defend and explain it. His description of his reaction on his mother's death is well known:

I was nearly thirteen when she died. My tutor and some other people scolded me for not mourning her. It so happened that I was reading some novels at that time and now and again would give a loud laugh. But secretly God softened my eyes into many tears which I did not wipe away with other people's handkerchiefs but with my own so that nobody was aware of them. (*Letters*, p. 26)

Similarly, Almqvist tried to explain other situations in which his seemingly cool behavior gave those around him the wrong impression. Thus, he says in a letter to his friend Wieselgren on October 14, 1837:

> One rarely has the good fortune to meet such friends when one comes to a strange place: I certainly have friends in all parts of the country but nowhere are they any warmer. I wish I could show all of you my warmth in return! but that is not possible. I am as it were closed up. (*Letters*, p. 122)

Again he writes to his old friend J. A. Hazelius in a famous letter in the fall of 1844:

> As for me, as soon as a conversation becomes heated, I immediately go cold, closed up, silent as a fish: except perhaps once in a while when I have become infected and lost my head in an outburst of my own, but this, I think, is strictly speaking, quite rare. I generally feel indescribably depressed and unhappy when the person I am talking to flares up in discussions; I look down at the floor, say little or nothing; as soon as possible I stop it all and try to get on to commonplace topics [. . .] A silent, cold reserve in anyone in the midst of other's tempestuous din presents a pretty hateful, or at least a demonic picture: if one can explain away the thing as stupidity or inability to reply, well and good, but if that is not credible the silence will be taken for inveterate surly obstinacy or subterfuge, falseness, cunning and deceit, at the very least it is uncommunicativeness. (*Letters*, p. 199 f.)

It is evident that what Almqvist says in "Dialogue on How to Finish Pieces" must apply partly to himself, partly to Tintomara. In other literary works as well he touches upon these traits; the protagonist of *Amorina*, for instance, cannot bring herself to show her grief openly at her mother's death and is consequently regarded as cold.

V   *Almqvist's Sources*

Before leaving *The Queen's Jewel*, we should say a few words about the sources Almqvist used. He made a detailed study of the historical setting and the events that had taken place forty years earlier.

From childhood he had had access to information, passed

down by oral tradition, concerning Gustavian times and particularly the assassination of the King. Almqvist's grandmother,
Birgitta Eleonora Gjörwell, was an important link; on her death
in 1822 her grandson wrote that she had been "of Gustav III's
period, and though she was only a poor librarian's wife, she had
also been very much liked by the King for her good manners"
(*Letters*, p. 45). And still more important, she had attended
the fateful masked ball. Almqvist's older friend and former
superior, the librarian Jacob Björkegren ("The Man Who Hated
God" in "The Hunting Seat") had been tutor to Ankarström,
the assassin of the King, and must certainly also have been
the transmitter of oral traditions about the murder. Ankarström's
widow, who did not die until 1844, was a half cousin to Almqvist's mother, and Almqvist''s father had known several of the
great men of the 1790s. Finally, it must be remembered that what
old Gjörwell, Almqvist's talkative and jovial grandfather, did
not know about the facts and the gossip of the last decades of
the eighteenth century was not worth knowing.

Oral tradition must have been important to Almqvist; and to
that must be added all the information he gleaned from a
thorough and systematic study of printed and unprinted sources.

In his monograph on *The Queen's Jewel*, Henry Olsson has
shown how the author studied the official reports of the trial
of the King's murderers in 1792 (Svea Court of Appeal Reports),
which he followed very closely in his novel.[4] In fact, in his
documentary zeal, Almqvist went so far as to insert long passages
from the various reports into the novel; this is especially the
case with the characterization of the assassin Ankarström. His
written confession is taken word for word from the reports
of the proceedings; the uncle who is fond of music reads aloud
from this document (*CW*, VI, pp. 187–92).

It will be recalled (see p. 80 above) that Richard Furumo
refers to the sources of his narrative. Documents relevant to the
trial are mentioned, and it has now been revealed that many
are authentic (for instance, those concerning the Ankarström
case). Thus, the occasional genuine document strengthens the
illusion of reality, which lends credibility to the other letters
which are entirely fictitious. The Ankarström case is one of
many examples.

To call Almqvist's work a documentary novel would be an exaggeration, of course, but there are striking documentary elements in *The Queen's Jewel*. From one point of view, these may be said to derive from the Romantic aesthetic theory of the novel with its trend toward mixed genres and forms of art. They can also be regarded as examples of Realism and an expression of Almqvist's growing longing for the poetry of facts. A parallel can also be drawn with the modern novel and its tendency toward documentation and anti-fiction.

CHAPTER 6

Swedish Fates and Southern Adventures

I Ramido Marinesco

*T*HE *Queen's Jewel* deals largely with passions, whether manifest in duels or double jealousies, as Richard Furumo says in his introduction. Almqvist takes up the theme of passion from a different and a rather less common angle in *Ramido Marinesco*. A short play in seven scenes (on the title page designated simply as "scenes"), it was published late in 1834 as Volume V of *The Book of the Wild Rose* (duodecimo edition).

Ramido Marinesco begins with a motto concerning the penitent Don Juan which is pronounced by Herr Hugo, and it ends with notes which also issue from Herr Hugo. In between is the actual play, allegedly recited by Richard Furumo.

Don Ramido, son of the legendary Don Juan, is compelled by his mother, Donna Bianca, to leave his home in Majorca (where he has been brought up by the learned monk, Anselmo) in order to win honor and love in Spain.

The four scenes following describe Ramido as he falls in love with four young women, one after the other, only to find that they are all daughters of the indefatigable Don Juan—and consequently Ramido's half sisters.

Disillusioned with life, Ramido returns to Majorca and devotes himself chiefly to the contemplation of a portrait (painted by Don Juan) representing a woman of exquisite beauty. Here at last he finds a "daughter" of Don Juan whom he can love. He kisses the picture, but this proves fatal, for Don Juan has amused himself by mixing poison into the paint.

> So I paint things, Donna Bianca,
> Just because it pleases me—

And Ramido dies. The monk, Anselmo, then reveals to Donna Bianca that he is Don Juan himself, but enduring penance, in duty bound to try to attract the hatred of those who once loved him:

> ANSELMO:
>> Who I am—so you do hate me?
>
> BIANCA:
>> That I swore and that I keep to
>> Nothing in your shape can make me
>> Feel regret at what I promised.
>> Take your mask off and your cowl,
>> Lift Anselmo, lift your hood. . . .
>> . . . .
>
> God! Oh, my black sun! . . . Don Juan! (*CW*, VII, p. 73)

With this uncanny revelation the play ends.

This variant of the Don Juan story combines several rewarding motifs: the father-son (or mother-son) motif, the incest motif, the motif of the poisoned portrait, the motif of the disguised penitent, the Galatea motif, etc.

The treatment of the story is itself inventive and original: the young man who continually falls in love with women who turn out to be his half sisters, and who finally becomes enamored of a picture which is also his father's handiwork and his own undoing: this is an interesting elaboration of the old tale.

Ramido himself, looking back, presents the story briefly in the following lines:

> I have fled, oh, Donna Bianca,
> From my father's many daughters,
> Now I love the woman, painted
> By Don Juan on that canvas.
> (*CW*, VII, p. 60)

The scene is set in a vaguely Renaissance milieu, in Majorca and a number of Spanish towns.

Almqvist has studied the setting thoroughly and of course there is something of a geography text in the enumeration of exotic trees and fruits provided by Ramido in his rapturous catalogue of the wonderful things in Señora Zia's garden in Valencia:

> A freshness under the mulberry branches,
> An aromatic fragrance in the shades of
> A thousand colors, vapors, vegetation
> Of olives, cedars, peaches, oranges
> And lemons, pastañetas, apricots,
> Pomegranates, citrons float enchantingly
> Around the happy wanderer in your Eden.
>
> (*CW*, VII, p. 22)

The catalogue technique reappears, for example, in the enumeration of exotic place-names by Donna Bianca:

> Look towards the sea, Anselmo,
> Do you see the isles: Yviza,
> Formentera, Conejera,
> Plañas, Cañas, Tagomagu,
> Espuntel, Espalmador?
>
> (*CW*, VII, p. 55)

It is easy to criticize, as many have, this piling up of exotic place-names, but there is a hint of magic and incantation in the reciting of the strange toponyms. Almqvist himself pointed out, e.g. *Människosläktets saga* (*The Saga of Mankind*), how place-names conjure up to our inner ear the sort of melody that floats mysteriously over land and people (p. 96).

The women Don Ramido meets were highly praised by Runeberg in his review of the play. On the other hand it must be admitted that the action is repetitive, as each new love scene ends in the discovery that the young woman is Don Juan's daughter.

The play was highly admired for its richly exotic and harmonious verse; but it was also criticized in contemporary reviews for what was "misty blue or half-explained" in the ending. As in the case of *The Queen's Jewel*, Almqvist answered his critics in his "Dialogue on How to Finish Pieces."

He also gave an important interpretation of Ramido's ill luck and death: Ramido dies at the climax of his experience of love and beauty. This is in full accord with Almqvist's view of death, murder, and suicide, as expressed in the Magdalena episode in "The Hunting Seat," the ending of *The Queen's*

Jewel (in which Tintomara is killed by the only person who
really loves her), and the *songe,* "The Drowned Swimmer"
(which was prompted by an actual suicide by two lovers whom
Almqvist knew well). Those who exchanged this life for the
one described by Swedenborg in *De Amore Conjugiali* and by
Almqvist in *Murnis,* had emerged triumphant.

Referring to the ending of the play quoted above (p. 90),
Almqvist makes the following defensive comment:

The piece ends, as is well known, at the very moment when
Bianca discovers that the Anselmo she has sworn to hate is none
other than her Don Juan. People have asked: What comes next?
What guarantee is there that she will keep her promise after this
discovery: and if she does not, what of the nemesis Don Juan
expects to face? My general answer to all this is that I do not
know.—I leave it to the reader to fill in the picture. (*CW,* VII, p. 209)

This is the aesthetics of collaboration which we have previously noted in connection with *The Queen's Jewel* and which
constitutes the central idea of the aesthetic treatise, "Dialogue
on How to Finish Pieces."

Like so many other of Almqvist's dramatic works, *Ramido
Marinesco* was never performed in public during the poet's
lifetime; it had to wait until the twentieth century.

II   *"Baron Julius K*"*

In 1835 two new volumes of *The Book of the Wild Rose*
were published in the duodecimo series, the sixth containing
"Baron Julius K*" and "Dialogue on How to Finish Pieces" and
the seventh with *Signora Luna* and *Colombine.*

It is typical of the rhythm and variation of the *Wild Rose*
series that Almqvist likes to pair off contrasting works. After
the exotic verse drama, *Ramido Marinesco,* with its profusion
of glaring southern colors and place-name poetry, comes the
gay rosy-cheeked travelogue "Baron Julius K*," with its Bieder-
meyer charm and its detailed description of a journey through
Östergötland and Västergötland.

"Baron Julius K*," bearing the subtitle "From Miss Eleonora's
Travel Reminiscences," describes a tour made by the engaged

couple Julianus and Aurora Löwenstjerna around Lake Vättern. They are accompanied and guided by Aunt Eleonora and a few members of the Hunting Seat circle—Frans, Henrik, and Richard Furumo. The company is joined, curiously enough, by one of the characters from a novel by Fredrika Bremer: Mademoiselle Angelika Rönnqvist. On the journey they meet the mysterious Baron Julius K*, who turns out to have been involved in a scandal concerning Andreas Löwenstjerna's matrimonial life and misfortunes, a matter which is dealt with in greater detail in *The Hind*. It is evident that "Baron Julius K*" is closely connected with that novel, and as has already been said, it is included in what is called "The Manor House Chronicle." Thus, the baron makes the acquaintance of the travelers, narrates, confesses, dies, bequeaths his property and his capital to Julianus, and leaves memoirs, parts of which are reproduced. The whole story ends solemnly in the manor chapel where the two young people are married.

"Baron Julius K*" for the most part conforms to the pattern of travel books, and Almqvist uses material from his own travel letters and notes from his journeys to Östergötland and Västergötland in 1827 and '29. One possible model is Laurence Sterne's *A Sentimental Journey*; Almqvist, however, is far less adventurous in his narrative technique and far more moral in his reflections.[1]

A central figure in "Baron Julius K*" is the narrator, Aunt Eleonora, of whom Almqvist gives a fine, sympathetic portrait. She is an unmarried, middle-aged woman who, like her brother, is endowed with kindness and common sense. She is alert and thirsty for knowledge; she exercises a quiet authority in her capacity as chaperone to the newly engaged couple on their travels.

At the beginning Herr Hugo states the objective of the young couple's journey:

To be married is to *travel through life together*. In order to see whether two persons are suited for a journey through life together, they should first make another ordinary journey through one or two provinces of the kingdom, because they will then come up against each other in so many different circumstances, see, notice, and

understand each other in so many different emotional states that
this journey will be the best means of discovering whether it is
feasible to embark upon the more important journey, marriage. The
trial journey had better be undertaken while they are engaged,
because then they are close enough to learn what they need to
know of each other; but not so close that they cannot separate if it
turns out that separation is better and that the great journey ought
to be abandoned. In my opinion all engaged couples ought to tour
the country once so as to be able to sit still and be nice to each
other once they are married. Now we see instead married couples
traveling around in order to disperse a cloud that they cannot in any
case remove because it hangs over every house and inn, every farmstead where they seek lodging. (*CW*, VII, p. 84–85)

And after the happy conclusion of the journey, it is Aunt
Eleonora who gives the young couple the wise advice:
"Behave during the whole of your married life as if you were
still unmarried, and everything will be all right" (*CW*, VII, p. 181).
Both Herr Hugo's opinion and Aunt Eleonora's more practical
advice anticipate the ideas of the important essay "*Varför reser
du?*" ("Why Do You Travel?"), where traveling is offered as a
pattern for living. We find a supplementary view of love and
marriage in Baron Julius K*'s posthumous papers:

When there is no pure, deep, and powerful feeling of heavenly
sympathy between two hearts—then the two beings do not live like
husband and wife as part of one another, and they are not united in
that way. Even if a third person's hand has blessed them, if his mouth
has spoken over them, these persons are still not so united that they
live in each other like husband and wife. (*CW*, VII, p. 171)

Here we find clearly stated already the problems to be discussed in *Sara Videbeck* and *The Causes of European Discontent*. Moreover, it is obvious that the travel book form, with
its delight in landscape and realistic detail, anticipates *Sara
Videbeck*; Aunt Eleonora, however, is not as emancipated in her
views of married and unmarried life as Sara Videbeck.
Feminism surfaces in "Baron Julius K*" in yet another way.
A discreet criticism of Fredrika Bremer's *The President's
Daughters* can be detected in Almqvist's work. Karin Westman

Berg points out that the learned governess, Angelika Rönnqvist (quite openly borrowed from Fredrika Bremer's novel), often gets the worst of it in her encounters with Aunt Eleonora's common sense and intuition. The same scholar also concludes that the social attitudes in "Baron Julius K*" indicate that Almqvist was not yet resolved to "take sides with the reformists concerning the emancipation of women whereas he was already cautiously beginning to question existing laws and ecclesiastical influence with regard to the contracting of marriage."[2]

However, in "Baron Julius K*" Almqvist was evidently beginning to move from death mysticism toward everyday problems and controversy. In the distance, Almqvist had heard the rumbling of the thunder which, in his own words, was threatening the age and which was to discharge itself through his pen in *The Causes of European Discontent.*

III   Signora Luna

In sharp contrast to the novel about an engagement trip around Lake Vättern follows a dire tragedy set in Sicily. This five-act drama, *Signora Luna*, was published in November 1835, together with *Colombine.*

The blind and saintly Signora Luna in her youth ran away with the formidable corsair, the Arab Abulkasem Ali Moharrem, and in so doing caused her parents to die of grief. However, Moharrem leaves her, and her two children are kidnapped and disappear. When the play begins, Signora Luna, sorely tried, is living in Palermo as a good, saintly benefactress, beloved of the people.

The ruler of the town is the tyrant Rinaldo, but the beautiful Princess Violanta of Messina is preparing a rebellion against him. She plans to murder the tyrant, but at the last moment saves his life. The victim and the would-be murderess fall in love with each other, but at their wedding an old pirate turns up and stabs Rinaldo. Violanta drops dead. Signora Luna, who has recovered her eyesight, can verify that the pirate is Moharrem, her missing husband, and further disclosures now follow in quick succession. It turns out that the two dead lovers are Moharrem's and her children. Luna grieves and dies.

Thus, a variant of the incest motif is combined with the foundling motif in this play. The complicated relationship between parents and children requires little comment. Olle Holmberg is of the opinion that the Italy that is presented in *Signora Luna*, with palace revolutions and assassinations, family tragedies and incests, is in keeping with the scenic-lyrical pieces of Byron and Victor Hugo, reinforced by elements out of straight melodrama.[3]

Almqvist spent much time on *Signora Luna*. Letters show that Atterbom had read the play in manuscript and proposed certain alterations.

The piece was read aloud seven times in Malla Silfverstolpe's salon over Christmas 1834 to, among others, "her assembled friends, the Geijers, Atterboms, Palmblads, not without comments from Geijer, who expressed himself with his usual impetuosity. He said, among other things: 'Now, now, one hears too much of the machinery.' "[4]

In a letter to Peter Wieselgren of January 23, 1836, Almqvist mentions *Signora Luna*, "which in its present shape contains the feelings of my heart and might be more eloquent than any letter to you." Algot Werin, referring to this letter, is of the opinion that *Signora Luna* casts light upon one aspect of the conversion to human concerns that took place in Almqvist in the middle of the 1830s.[5]

Signora Luna does not want to be revered as a saint, she is a human being who knows what sorrow and crime are:

> the shining light does not last
> Soon it will be tinged with earthly twilight,
> By sorrow, wishes, grief, and somber pain
> From white to red, to blue it changes into—black!
> My inner light is colored by the faults
> Of my own heart, by crimes—   (*CW*, VII, p. 351)

This is stressed by Richard Furumo in his introduction, when he answers Herr Hugo:

Here we see a human being who, by nature and as the result of misfortune, already stands high: who at the very beginning of the scenes is at a peak—but who thereafter descends, moves further and further down toward her fellow men, is constricted, concentrated and contracted into an individual of ordinary dimensions. In other words it is the humanizing of a saintly character which, to my mind, is reflected here. Can you solve the riddle, Herr Hugo, and tell me if this is as it should be, if it is noble? if it is noble enough on earth to be a human being, and no more? (*CW*, VII, p. 234)

This is the same dilemma as that faced by the artist in "The Poet's Night" when, at the end of his reflection, he longs to come down to the level of human beings: "God—my God— this is my last appeal to you: let me also wither away and die like the others."

IV Colombine

If *Signora Luna* shows the humanization of a saint, then it can be said that *Colombine* is the canonization of a sinner.

Colombine, subtitled "The Story of the Dove from Scania," was printed after *Signora Luna*, to which it affords a well-calculated contrast, in the seventh volume of *The Book of the Wild Rose*.

"I will tell you what virtue is like," says the young Count Fredrik in the opening line to the pure-hearted prostitute, Colombine, during a profound conversation at a brothel. He then proceeds to instruct her on the voice of pure virtue, which is "the only voice that is heard and felt in the depth of the soul of society" (*CW*, VII, p. 391, 395).

Fredrik runs away with Colombine, breaks with his fiancée and falls out with his family. His father, the blunt old Count, feels a certain pride initially in his son's resolute behavior, and says as much to his other son, Jakob, who is all too soft and obsequious. The Count has a great scene with Jakob, which is one of the liveliest in Swedish drama prior to Strindberg.

Fredrik and Colombine go to Scania, where by a woodland spring they encounter a poor organist and his wife, who turn out to be Colombine's parents (from whom she was stolen at the age of three). Colombine is purged of her sinful past by being taught by a priest and then confirmed. In the final scene, Count Fredrik leads Colombine from the confirmation ceremony to the place where they are to be married.

Certain familiar motifs are evident: the motif of the pure-hearted prostitute, the uniting of the man of noble birth with the woman of the people, the father-son relationship, and the conflict between brothers.

The theme of the whole work is announced in Count Fredrik's opening words: virtue and marriage are the subject of the drama. It is obvious that Almqvist is himself passing through a personal crisis, and documents from the day confirm this. But at the same time, he takes a cheerfully defensive attitude. *Colombine* shows an Almqvist who is increasingly attentive to new reformist political goals but who has not yet begun his forward march. After *Colombine* Almqvist was silent as an aesthetic and political writer for nearly three years. It was not until the end of 1838 that new volumes of *The Book of the Wild Rose* appeared in the bookshops.

It goes without saying that the noble Count Fredrik and the pure-hearted beauty, Colombine, are the principal characters of the piece as far as action and dialogues are concerned. But there is a third dominant figure: namely, Fredrik's father, the blunt old Count, who adjures his pious son Jakob with fiery oaths:

"Devils in hell—Jakob—you must have respect for God" (*CW*, VII, p. 406).

One oft-quoted passage is the conversation with Jakob during which the Count extols the virtues of the Vikings and deplores the decline of Swedish manliness:

The Vikings were my people and we are probably descended from them. Mark my words: a mercenary mind, wretched scruples, ignoble calculations, and a baseness which leads nowhere—that's what we have come to, and so far as I can see, there's as little honor in it as profit. What the devil do they achieve with all their calculating? Do they accomplish anything? Oh, it is hell to see and a shame to hear. If the Lord didn't from time to time send a sound character, like me for instance, to give some things a good shake up, the world would get eaten up by moths. (*CW*, VII, p. 415 f.)

There is a mixture of parody and seriousness in the brilliant portrait of the old Count. Almqvist has skillfully juxtaposed the Count's supercilious attitude and choleric historical romanticism to Fredrik's and Colombine's social and religious aspirations.

Almqvist himself valued *Colombine* highly from several points of view. He has commented on this piece as well as on others in an important letter to Wieselgren of February 15, 1836:

What I particularly enjoy is describing persons and events in various parts of the world, where I can paint scenery and people, everything, with the various shades of color, tone, and modes of expression that make up their individualism. Thus I have composed a short piece, *Ramido Marinesco*, in which action, characters, and surroundings—all—are Spanish (in the Valencian mode): another, "Arthur's Hunt," is British, although not in the modern English fashion but from ancient Celtic times:—another, *Ninon de Lenclos*, is French, dealing with Parisian life in the seventeenth century. The varying metrical rhythms help greatly toward the individualization. (Thus, *Ninon*, for instance, is written in alexandrines, though light and airy: *Arthur* in primitive lyric meter: *Ramido* has Spanish elegiac forms:—the first two works have not been printed yet)—You may well now ask me if there is anything typically *Swedish*? *Colombine* gives the feel of Sweden. (*Letters*, p. 101 f.)

Thus, until the advent of "The Significance of Swedish Poverty," Almqvist lets *Colombine* represent the Swedish character and Swedish sentiment.

V *Ordination. Pause*

During the first few years after 1835, Almqvist was feverishly active in other fields. He studied theology at Uppsala and was ordained in 1837. Malla Silfverstolpe, who attended his ordination, said that she did not like his looks when he took the clerical oath. "It seemed to me as if it were to him only an empty formula without inner significance or strength."[6] And another eyewitness, Rudolf Hjärne, noticed that, during the very act, Almqvist "turned around and let his eyes wander uneasily all around the church, as if his imagination had taken possession of his soul and transported it far away from the place and from what was being enacted there."[7]

As already stated, Almqvist also applied for another post, the professorship of aesthetics and modern languages at Lund.

He spent a few weeks there in the fall of 1838, also paying a short visit to Denmark.

In addition he had been busy writing his *Greek Grammar*, which, upon publication in 1837, became the object of a scathing review by Palmblad that lead to a polemic between the two former friends.

During these three years, Almqvist consolidated his political beliefs and commitments.

Late in 1838, Almqvist left Lund for Stockholm and—still hoping to obtain the academic post—brought out a number of new items for *The Book of the Wild Rose*.

CHAPTER 7

From Asiatic Exotism to Swedish Poverty

I "Araminta May"

THE new series of *Wild Rose* books begins in December
1838 with the short dialogue "Återkomsten" ("The Return") and its confident announcement of forthcoming artistic
projects.

The very title alludes discreetly to the long interruption in
the publication of *The Book of the Wild Rose,* and in the introductory lines, Herr Hugo welcomes Richard Furumo back to
the Hunting Seat after a long journey.

This time the conversation ranges over the common qualities
of epic and drama, a fruitful subject that Almqvist has touched
on several times before (p. 39). In "The Return," Almqvist
has Richard Furumo introduce, among other works, the short
epistolary story, "Araminta May," stressing its comic character.

It has sometimes seemed to me that letters exchanged between
persons bear resemblance to *conversations*: it is like a dramatic
dialogue taking place at a distance between those concerned. They
don't exchange spoken words but written lines. If you should feel
like comparing my collection of letters here to a drama, Herr
Hugo, I have no objection. (*CW*, VIII, p. 6)

This notion of the dramatic nature of correspondences coincides with views expressed by a number of important novelists
and theorists of the novel, beginning with Richardson and
Blankenburg.

After discussing comedy and tragedy, Richard Furumo proceeds to look beyond the conventional classification into genres.
If a work is happy,

then I would not object to giving it the name of *comedy* even though the piece is written in the form of a *narrative*. Actions (acts), pictures (scenes), and conversation (dialogues)—I have no objection: but not arranged and divided up for the stage, rather for the inner eye of an unseeing listener, the eye of the soul before which a great spectacle, nay, one of the very greatest, is performed, and perhaps to the best advantage. (*CW*, VIII, p. 7)

Such comedies not "visibly divided into acts and scenes" are, for example, "Araminta May," and also "The Palace," "The Chapel," "Skällnora Mill," and *Sara Videbeck*.

Richard Furumo insists vigorously on the interrelationship of the dramatic and epic forms of art, defending himself against possible objections by his listeners that the canons of art would become confused and that no fixed definition could be maintained; that epic would merge into drama and vice versa. "To this I could answer that modern times have constricted and limited the concept of each genre, decreed unnecessary distinctions and subdivisions, in a word, erected partitions purely for the sake of having a stable. But aesthetic stables—whatever for?" (*CW*, VIII, p. 8).

Consequently "Araminta May," subtitled "A visit to Grönhamn Deanery," is presented on the title page as "a correspondence"; it is a story in letter form, or a short epistolary novel. It is read to the Hunting Seat circle by Richard Furumo, as is evident from the concluding lines of "The Return."

The letter writers are Fabian, a young Stockholm wholesaler, and Henriette, his beautiful cousin, both representatives of the merchant upper class. Fabian is in the country hoping to find a wife from among the deanery daughters at Grönhamn. In detail, he reports his increasingly less enthusiastic impressions of the inner qualities and outer appearances of the provincial graces. Henriette, his confidante, invents the portrait of a charmingly coquettish friend, Araminta May, with whom Fabian falls head over heels in love by letter. Finally it is disclosed that the mysterious and charming Araminta is actually Henriette, who reveals herself as a "lovely liar." Fabian and Henriette are united on the basis thus defended by Fabian:

If there are burdens in life, as I believe there will be, may you make me regard them as light by saying their weight is not heavy.

What an untruth! But that's how the world goes. And should things become too riotously merry around us, may you make me believe that something sad lurks there: then we shall have the proper measure of happiness. Henriette! who could stand the dark of the night if we didn't tell lies to form rays around the stars? And who could stand the bright sun of day without wrapping himself up in some refreshing shade? The *shade* itself . . . is there anything more inexplicable? Anything less tangible? It is nothing and nonetheless it exists. It is, I believe, the very "coquetry" of the earth with its own realities. However, it is quite wrong of me to call all this lies. Such as you have been and still are, Henriette, as you have written and acted, you show me the very truth: the best, perhaps the highest truth of life. (*CW*, VIII, p. 74 f.)

Thus, the final scene of "Araminta May" contains, among many other things, a discreet defense of the value and role of illusion, and the narrator's use of shade or shadow as a symbol and metaphor reminds us of Almqvist's contemporary, Hans Andersen.

"Araminta May" has a charming comic atmosphere, light as gossamer. Scholars have compared it with Marivaux's comedies as well as Musset's *Comédies et proverbes*.[1] The epistolary style is finely and delicately matched to the mentalities, temperaments, sexual roles, and passing moods. As early as 1832, in his Swedish grammar, Almqvist had "given proof of the easy and fluent epistolary style that he employs with such artistry in *The Queen's Jewel* and 'Araminta May'" (*CW*, VIII, p. ix).

These two works can be compared in other respects as well. Both are rightly famous as lovingly drawn descriptions of Stockholm, accurate down to the smallest topographical detail. In both, too, are strong elements of masquerade and qui pro quo. But "Araminta May" is a less dangerous, sanguinary masquerade than the frightening, deadly earnest one in *The Queen's Jewel*.

After this gay, witty, epistolary comedy set in and around idyllic, contemporary Stockholm, we are offered a short story, "The Urn," which takes place in medieval Germany.

The ingredients, a strong decoction of historical romance, follows:

On her wedding night Aldegunda von Rheinstetten swears a solemn oath before her husband Mauritz von Hochmanswaldau that in the event of his death, she will weep over his ashes and fast for seven days.

After some time, a message arrives announcing that her husband has died, and an urn with his ashes is brought to Aldegunda, who faithfully fulfills her promise. After a year she marries again, but on the wedding night Mauritz appears, kills the bridegroom, and burns down the castle. To the amazed Aldegunda, Mauritz points out that she has broken her oath as it was not *his* ashes she had wept over; he also tells her that he has carried out this infernal plan deliberately. He then shuts her up in a gigantic alabaster urn to be buried alive.

Many years pass. Mauritz, an old man on his deathbed, confesses that he has committed a fraud: before locking up Aldegunda, out of pity, he had poisoned her. The scene finishes very effectively with the dying man aware of the flames of hell licking around his bed.

In a letter to Lénström dated January 29, 1839, Almqvist explained the story and accentuated its essential point. "The urn contains the image of a man (Mauritz) in deep disharmony with himself as a result of the terrible obsession with the oath" (*Letters*, p. 141). Thus, the significance of the oath is the subject of the story. Almqvist shows how the consequences of an oath are pursued *ad absurdum* when Aldegunda is punished though she had been deliberately deceived and though she was convinced that she had kept her oath.

Algot Werin draws a comparison with the argument about the oath in *The Causes of European Discontent*. It is his opinion that the story of "The Urn," about the absurd consequences of an oath, relates biographically and psychologically to Almqvist's own thoughts on the clerical vow which had been prompted by his ordination in 1837 (*CW*, VIII, p. xiii).

II *"The Chapel"*

The short story "The Chapel," subtitled "A Day," was published together with "The Palace" in the ninth volume of *The Book of the Wild Rose* (duodecimo edition).

The plot follows:

On his first mission a young curate leaves Kalmar for Southern

Möre on the east coast of Sweden. He preaches in a little chapel on the fringe of the archipelago to elderly poor people; faced with this congregation, dealt with so harshly by life, he abandons the draft of his conventional prepared sermon and speaks simply and directly to his listeners. "He spoke both warmly and with moderation; he spoke as among friends." After the service he goes with Elin, the poor fisherman's wife, to her home and joins her and her children in their Sunday activities. The fishing fleet comes in with the message that Jonas, Elin's husband, has been drowned, and the curate stays to comfort them in their grief. But the sorrow is not long-lived, for Jonas has not been drowned but instead comes home a wealthy man. And so the day passes, and the curate says good-bye and leaves the little chapel community.

In an epilogue we learn that, in due course, the curate returns, marries Elin's and Jonas's eldest daughter and settles down in the archipelago which "often of rough, rugged, bare, and terrible aspect, enjoys a pleasant gentle breeze in several of its hidden little coves, and the smile of summer lingers on behind the cliffs" (*CW*, VIII, p. 152).

"The Chapel" was very probably inspired by Almqvist's ordination, and he undoubtedly endows the young clergyman with traits of a church reformer, possibly such as he would have liked to be himself. It has also been established that Almqvist's letters from his Småland journey in 1836 contain material for the short story and that certain passages in the letters were followed very closely in the fine descriptions of scenery.

The congregation, feeble with age and infirmity, is also described with searching realism, leaving a clear, sharp impression:

"He was deeply moved as well as frightened at the sight of all the surrounding figures: very long-chinned, pale, bald, or lank-haired, red-eyed or half-blind, either with pointed noses or extremely snub-nosed, most of them stooping but with great, clumsy hands, men and women alike, probably due to their occupation" (*CW*, VIII, p. 113 f.).

Kurt Aspelin finds an advanced technique in the composition of the sermon scene, which describes parallel events on different levels. He discusses the fundamental contrast between the flowery prose of the original sermon that the curate had intended to deliver and the lively, earnest, realistic sermon that he does deliver and relates this contrast to one of Almqvist's most important aesthetic works, "On the Poetry of Facts" (1839); the sermon scene becomes an artistic expression of the contrast between the poetry of facts and the poetry of mere words, which Almqvist discusses in his essay.[2] The story can also be linked with another of Almqvist's finest essays, namely, "The Significance of Swedish Poverty." Poverty, contentedness, but also the gift of accepting wealth and good fortune, are—according to Almqvist— Swedish characteristics; these are all demonstrated in "The Chapel." It is an austere but sunny idyll.

III *"The Palace" and* The Saga of Mankind.

After the windswept idyll of "The Chapel," Almqvist leaves Sweden's poverty for the Asiatic exotism of the story, "The Palace."

By the first log fire of the fall, the Hunting Seat circle come together on a fine cold evening to listen to "The Palace," a deftly composed tale which might well be compared to a detective story. Its brilliant, mysterious opening was clearly under the influence of E. T. A. Hoffmann, as was the overall atmosphere of the work. It is Richard Furumo who tells what he has personally witnessed. On a journey he arrives at an English seaport where, under mysterious circumstances, he is summoned to witness as an old Japanese man commits hara-kiri. In vain, Richard tries to stop the man; in vain he tries to save the old man's daughters who, in obedience to their father's patriarchal authority, are to follow him unto death. The mysterious palace where these exotic rites are carried out is finally burned down like a magnificent funeral pyre for the dead, and the narrator has a narrow escape.

The story is a thrilling tale of adventure set in a brilliantly described exotic milieu.

To Atterbom, Almqvist wrote on January 27, 1839:

The attractive, lovely, and captivating qualities that one may find in mere *speech sounds* without even knowing the sense they represent but only hearing them as notes, as musical sounds ... this idea is introduced in "The Palace," where beautiful, innocent female savages speak words that the listener cannot translate and thereby understand, but which he nevertheless appreciates because of the accompanying facial expressions, the charm of the voices, and the beauty of the sounds? Isn't that idea worth something? I've experienced the wonderfully interesting effect of it myself. Besides, if one knows Japanese life, Shintoism and the whole peculiar, and in *its own* characteristic way, chivalrous mood that pervades this nation, and Kubo's (the ruler's) wonderful empire, and the pattern of thought and so-called prejudices persisting among them, then one will find the whole of this work natural and interesting. (*Letters*, p. 138)

Here we find the Romantic attention to sound relating to music and which is also associated with the aesthetics of suggestion and fragment, already discussed.

But ethnographic and social problems are also emphasized. We must recall that during this period Almqvist was occupied with his great historical-geographic work, *The Saga of Mankind* (1839), the first and only volume of which bears the subtitle, *Greater Asia or the Inner Orient in Ancient and Modern Times*. In this work there are several passages that express his delight in foreign speech sounds. One of these is the fine disquisition on what we might appropriately call place name poetry (cf. p. 91).

The Saga of Mankind also includes a polemic on patriarchy in the section dealing with Chinese literature. In an interesting note, which can be taken as a comment on the theme of "The Palace," Almqvist launches a vehement attack on the principle of patriarchy. Twice two are four and not seven.

But if patriarchy is the *principle*, it follows that if one's forefathers have decreed that one shall believe that twice two are seven, then *their descendants are bound* to think so and act accordingly. It is certainly both possible and true that no fathers have decreed to their offspring the proposition we have taken as an example; but they have, in most cases with the best of intentions, taught and decreed what is nevertheless analogous to $2 \times 2 = 7$. Having to obey this is a result of patriarchy when it is the principle. Shall we do so, must we or may we do so? No. Consequently, patriarchy as a principle must fail. (*The Saga of Mankind*, p. 413)

The above serves as a direct commentary on what happens in "The Palace," but Almqvist gives further examples:

> When a mother, with religious fervor, but a torn heart, throws her child into the flames of Moloch's altar since Syrian priests have made it a sacred duty for her so to do: [...] this act offers a picture to the *poet*, attractive in a pure and pathetic, by no means satirical, sense. But the *philosopher* will not say: this was rightly done. (*The Saga of Mankind*, p. 413 ff.)

Almqvist gives the complex of problems a contemporary relevance and shows how common they are, not only in private but also in public life. The main point of the novel is: must one obey, and obey in everything? This is how Almqvist expresses himself in a letter to Lénström of January 29, 1839, about "The Palace":

> "The Palace"—when one sees it in its Asiatic-Japanese context as one should—has a fairly coherent inner consistency. The fact that Japanese noblemen disembowel themselves on the Emperor's (Kubo's) account is well known. The man in the piece who dies with his two daughters falls a victim to the horrible misconception that one must obey in *everything*. (*Letters*, p. 141)

As a matter of fact, Almqvist had done a draft of a separate essay on patriarchy and a parallel might be drawn with the privileges of the Swedish aristocracy of the period which, to the poet, seemed as absurd as those of the Japanese (for instance, in the latter's right to commit hara-kiri).[3]

In his reformist writings at the time of *The Saga of Mankind*, Almqvist took up such phenomena as "The Academic Patriarchy" in his great survey of the Swedish educational system, and in the 1840s his impassioned journalism included a violent attack on the prerogatives of both the aristocracy and the higher clergy.

But to revert to "The Palace," the tense, thrilling atmosphere of this excellent story, with its relatively simple, logical final solution and its clear thesis, makes it a comprehensive and entertaining work of art. It has also been interpreted symbolically: the burning palace is despotism, which deserves to perish in the fire of the universal revolution. Thus we see, in 1838, another indication of Almqvist's changed attitude toward practical politics.

Volume X of *The Book of the Wild Rose* contains *Godolphin or the Three Mr. Beaumanoirs*, "The Significance of Swedish Poverty," and "The Poet's Night." The first two pieces, in particular, contrast strongly with each other. *Godolphin*, subtitled "drama," is a comedy written mainly in alexandrines, and its subject matter is Parisian high society of the seventeenth century.

The dazzlingly beautiful and highly cultivated courtesan, Ninon de l'Enclos, has all of Paris at her feet, but she fails to bewitch Henri Beaumanoir, a young misogynist from the provinces. For him she is too much art and too little nature. The one who incarnates nature is Jasmée, a pretty young woman from the provinces, "a plain rose from Dauphiné," and Henri prefers her. At the end of the last act, however, Ninon discloses that *she* is actually also Jasmée whose part she played to Henri. Thus far the motif is really the same as that presented in Henriette's disguise in "Araminta May." The later part of the two works differs, however, for Henri leaves Ninon and Paris. The question of whether or not Ninon will follow him to Dauphiné as Jasmée is left open. The story of a will is also woven into the action.

Victor Hugo's dramas and Marivaux's comedies have been regarded as models for *Godolphin*.[4] But Almqvist makes even more out of it. In his concluding notes we encounter the line of argument of *The Causes of European Discontent*, which occupied Almqvist at the time of this writing. All "false duties" should be banned and no harmful letters contrary to nature laid on moral human life. This is more important than anything else: "When this is deeply and generally understood, it will bring about a revolution in education more important than the sharp turn in modern politics." In fact these notes are sometimes identical with drafts of the great socio-political treatises that survive among Almqvist's papers (*CW*, VIII, p. xxvii).

Thus, Almqvist created for this piece, too, a frame consisting of an "Introduction" and a postscript (in dialogue form entitled "Notes"). In the introduction, Richard Furumo, Herr Hugo, and Julianus discuss the subject and title of Richard's "drama." There are interesting echoes of the aesthetic conversations in "The Return." Richard talks about scenes "to be shown in every listener's interior theater, the lively stage of imagination, well set up, rich in splendid scenery and provided with excellent actors and actresses (feelings and thoughts)" (*CW*, VIII, p. 207).

The concluding notes have yet another function: namely, to provide the epic situation for his next work, "The Significance of Swedish Poverty."

IV *The Significance of Swedish Poverty*

The crown of the *Wild Rose* books of 1838 is the brilliant essay, "The Significance of Swedish Poverty," written in the spring of that year. This piece occupies a distinguished central place in the succession of descriptions of Swedish national character from Stiernhielm to Heidenstam.

Almqvist begins by raising the question of the relationship between the different classes in Sweden, between gentlefolk and peasantry. His intention is to write for the common people, but then, he says, the paradox arises: Who will read and understand his thoughts? The gentlefolk can read but do not understand or do not want to understand; the common people would understand but cannot read. How can this be explained?

The upper classes have become unnational; their culture has taken quite a different course from that of the nation. "Their studies are scarcely Swedish. Their raptures are foreign. They eat and sleep in Sweden; but their breasts draw their fondest breaths in Germany or France, sometimes in England" (*CW*, VIII, p. 301). But the worst of it is that these people do not feel like Swedes, that is why one of their number lacks "the national peculiarity, the individual shading that would make him an interesting *person*" (*CW*, VIII, p. 301). Against the Classicists' demands for the universal, Almqvist poses the Romantics' preference for what is individually interesting.

The common people get no help from the gentlefolk; on the contrary, the two classes are drifting further and further apart. Almqvist's reflections have already acquired a political tinge: "The peasant and his master go different and conflicting ways in their spiritual development, they do not love each other at heart, they misunderstand each other thoroughly, and *would perhaps betray each other in the hour of need* if such a time should ever come" (*CW,* VIII, p. 306; my italics). In order to avoid such a gloomy prospect, the two parties must be united by learning what is characteristic of the nation, what is Swedish.

The first part of the essay that follows might have been called, "What is the national, the Swedish character?" This question is difficult to answer, such things cannot be taught, "because it is hardly rational. It resides chiefly in feeling." So go out and get to know your people and your country: "Look at the bright-green leaves that our trees bear, they are not succulent or dark-green like those of the South—our real love in this country does not spring from lust but rather from coolness: from poverty, loneliness, and sometimes want from soul and heaven" (*CW,* VIII, p. 310).

In these words the poverty theme has been introduced, and Almqvist states that the Swede differs from all other peoples in being destined for poverty. "Being poor means being thrown upon one's own resources." That is the Swede's lot; but note that Almqvist hastens to stress that poverty is not something to aim at: it is in itself inhuman (witness the Spartans and the Jesuits). But rather than faculty for being *poor,* for managing by means of skill, independence, contentment, and resourcefulness: this gift is the basis of the Swedish national character.

The next major section of the essay could be entitled, "The Swede, Poverty, and Wealth." Here Almqvist discusses the proud Swedish indifference to wealth and possessions, "this resilience of temperament, this sinewy 'away from all possessions' [...] Clumsy as a speculator he is usually happiest when he goes bankrupt, and he deals more expeditiously with his creditors than he did with his merchandise" (*CW,* VIII, p. 317 f.).

The Swedish weakness is misunderstanding the real significance of poverty and despairing of developing what lies within one's self and in one's country.

The last part of the essay, the best known, deals with "Sweden, the Swedish character, and its Symbols." Almqvist takes his first set of symbols from the fauna: Sweden's wild animals, fishes, and birds—with their lively, playful, swift, shy movements—"are not only physical creatures in our country;

but—mark well—they are also patterns and figurations of the Swedish character." Swiftness and playfulness are also typical of the *horse*, which contrasts favorably with other domestic animals symbolizing other qualities less valuable in Almqvist's eyes. We find examples of the latter in his brilliantly amusing reflections on the serious ox, with the dignity of a bureaucrat, and the muddleheaded cow.

The horse is the animal that is closest to Almqvist's heart: "In the .ox we saw earthly profit and order followed for their own sake; but the horse stands for higher and noble enjoyment which brings as much benefit though in the form of pecuniary gain but rather as a delightful adjunct to life" (*CW*, VIII, p. 333).

But it is from the flora that Almqvist chooses his most beautiful symbol of what is Swedish: the briar rose, the Nordic wild rose:

Look at its simple, small, pink flower and inhale the fine, faint fragrance, the noblest, however, that the air carries. Here there is no lush rich foliage; not the succulent bright-red southern briar rose, reminiscent of passion; nor the strong narcotic vapor, sister of amber, musk, and all manner of oriental incense. During its short flowering the wild rose bush does indeed display a goodly number of small few-petaled flowers; it is tall though slender, and it has quite as many thorns as its southern or eastern relatives. But it is the picture of poverty, wild grace, and chastity. It represents the whole of our Nordic landscape, concentrated in a phantom. (*CW*, VIII, p. 334)

A brief conclusion again contrasts the North and the South. In the North the seasons are not favorable to flowers, the temperate months are too few; but it may be the long winters in Sweden that keep land and people young. In a rapid calculation—that Gothicists, not to mention Montesquieu, would have appreciated—Almqvist compares the Northerners and the Southerners. Thanks to the mild climate, the latter live through ten months of growth each year whereas the Swede has only four or five. Thus, Almqvist concludes cheerfully, the Swede is always half as old as the Southerner, and consequently twice as young, and the closing words are a song of praise to the winter:

The same season that invites the southern European to sit over his wine, drinking merrily or chatting heartily with relatives and guests about everything that is profitable and polite: that same season invites the Swede to go sledging or skating, to chop wood or to sleep. Is it so strange then that he remains young? But the former must be a staid man, well versed in the whole alphabet of life.

But since it happens to be our lot in the world to go sledging, let us do so. When a jolly girl sits on the sledge and a young man on skates pulls it, they are away in a flash. I like that. Why shouldn't I boast a little of the North? (*CW*, VIII, p. 341)

The thought and the theme of the essay is that poverty is the key to the destiny of Sweden and the Swedish character: from this poverty emanate all the qualities that are most inimitably Swedish. Being poor means being thrown upon one's own resources, it means being self-reliant, alert, independent, indefatigable in adversity; it also means being indifferent to property and wealth, lighthearted, nay, almost irresponsible.[5]

In terms of the history of ideas, we find the same brand of patriotism as in the documents of Manhemsförbundet. Almqvist certainly reacts against the more extreme manifestation of the Gothic movement:

It is not a question of the names Odin, Tor, Frigga, Nore, Svea—whether they appear in verses, on stagecoaches, or on a steamer. I see no reason why they should be excluded from our poetry if they are necessary for the character of the piece. But they are not much use if the character is missing. [. . .] Thus, the Swedish character does not consist of eccentricity, archeological dustiness, affected dullness, or a sort of patriotic rigidity and assertiveness—it conconsists of being Swedish rather than shouting that one is Swedish. (*CW*, VIII, p. 310 f.)

But on the other hand influences from Geijer and Montesquieu are quite obvious, notably in the consistently maintained contrast between South and North and the reflections on plants and climates. However, it is important that Almqvist's nationalism in this work has no historical perspective; it is not bound by tradition, and it is modern. It aims at depicting the living national character and the life of the common people.

In connection with Almqvist's opinion of the peasant class, we are reminded that he was influenced at an early stage—in his Värmland period—by the ideas of Rousseau; he maintained his preference for the idyllic life of the peasant. Böök observes in passing that Almqvist has "a veil of religious ecstasy between himself and reality that is the only explanation of his attributing to the Swedish peasantry indifference to property and a high-minded disregard of economic interests."[6]

Politically, Almqvist clearly reveals himself as a democrat and a liberal. He ignores the annals, the kings, and the upper classes and turns his attention to the lower strata of the population. In principle, he rates the peasant class higher than the upper classes. Almqvist wants to write for the people and says explicitly that he knows that he has an important task to perform. He frequently draws attention to the gap between the ruling classes and the people. If the two classes do not draw closer together, there is a risk of the state collapsing. Henrik Schück has pointed out that Almqvist's essay is far more democratic than the articles that Geijer wrote at the same time, after what was called his "desertion."[7]

The description of the peculiarities of the Swedish temperament, however, is chiefly self-characterization; it is Almqvist who feels that he himself is "in need of grace even in money matters." At this time he was beset by financial and other difficulties; but he was also full of vigor, playfulness, and confidence. We find an apt characterization of him in the description of the horse, "full of grace, fun, and wit." The ox, however, stands for all that is respectable, orderly, and timid: in other words, here we find the distinction between Ariman and Ormus.

Almqvist continued his program in his fine ethical tract, *Arbetets ära (The Nobility of Work)*, in the popular books, and in the pictures of everyday life, which will be considered later. The merry, dancing, poor fishermen's children in "The Chapel" clearly illustrate the theme of the essay, and economic as well as democratic sense are qualities of the principal persons in *Sara Videbeck*; Almqvist has provided an excellent counterpart in the short essay, "Why Do You Travel?" which will be treated later.

The tenth volume of *The Book of the Wild Rose* concludes

with the lyrical prose monologue, "The Poet's Night," also
discussed above (p. 52 f.).

V "Skällnora Mill"

The eleventh and last of the four new volumes of *The Book
of the Wild Rose* with which Almqvist surprised the public
in December 1838 contains "Skällnora Mill," a brilliantly narrated crime story with the style of the rustic tale and the mode
largely filled with Romantic horror. The plot follows:

A young traveling enthusiast from Stockholm tells about the
time he was on a walking tour in Uppland and met a young
peasant girl, Brita, on her way to Skällnora Mill with a cartload
of corn. The narrator follows her to Skällnora, and there by
mere chance he overhears a conversation between the miller
and the villainous Jan Carlson: the talk is about poisoning and
a certain plot against Brita. In terms of its development, the
story follows the crime story formula, the narrator being a
diligent but not very clever private detective. It appears that
Jan Carlson wanted to get rid of his sister and his brother-in-law
(who has Brita in his service) by poisoning his sister and
blaming her husband. It is uncertain whether or not his sister
died from poisoning, but Jan Carlson evidently regards himself
as her murderer. In order to carry out his plan and cast suspicion
on his brother-in-law, he now tries to force Brita to give false
evidence. At the sawmill, the narrator, unable to intervene,
is obligated to watch how Jan Carlson ties Brita to the log
close to the saw-blades and starts the machinery. While Jan
is trying to persuade Brita, he slips and falls into the rapids
and is killed. Only a *deus ex machina* in the form of a bird
manages to stop the saw: it pushes a chip in between the
saw teeth.

After this miraculous rescue the narrator and Brita part, and
the former proceeds on his journey.

Contemporary reviews and later research have unanimously
praised Brita, the principal female character; there is "something of the transient, lovely, northern spring flowering about
her."[8] There is also a distinctly Hoffmannesque atmosphere
over much of the tale, and in spite of the all-too-obvious contri-

vance, suspense is compellingly maintained and the setting brilliantly executed.

In this letter to Lénström of January 1839, Almqvist makes a "dissection" of "Skällnora Mill." It is an analysis which is very instructive in spite of its apologetic tone. Almquist presents a clear account of the plot and the development of the story, the construction of which he compares to that of a tragedy:

This piece is also (even though not divided into acts and scenes) in one important respect a tragedy in the proper sense of the word. Ever since Aristotle people had accustomed themselves to the strange opinion that only distinguished persons, kings, princes, heroes, queens, or at least noblemen must be the subject of the tragedy. I find that *man,* in any class of society, can be that. Here we have the peasant *Jan Carlson. (Letters,* p. 132 f.)

The story is brought to a close by the *deus ex machina* in the form of a bird. Almqvist's comments upon the bird, however, raise the question of whether Jan Carlson's soul may not have flown into this bird, wishing to make amends for the evil deed he has committed.

Now, if a reader sees the bird in that way, he will be admitted into the higher mysteries of the piece; on the other hand, if he sees it *only* as a bird, there will be nothing wrong in that. Then it is a story of which the ending is deserved in that the villain falls a victim to his own machinations: then one need not look any further, that is sufficient. It is exactly as when, in the Aristotelian or old French tragedy, a *tyrant,* at the very height of his power and just about to achieve his final objective, is stabbed by a dagger that he carries *himself. (Letters,* p. 132 f.)

It is evident from what has been said that Almqvist, in his comments on the ending of the story, allows for the reader's choice of interpretation; the aesthetic doctrines enunciated in "Dialogue on How to Finish Pieces" are still valid. It may also be pointed out that Almqvist liked to comment upon his own works of fiction and analyze them in letters—as here—and publicly in newspapers and printed articles.[9]

With the above-mentioned critic, C. J. Lénström, associate

professor in Uppsala, Almqvist carried on an intensive correspondence for some years. Lénström, who edited the literary review *Eos* from 1839 to 1840, was a person easily influenced in his enthusiasms, and Almqvist was not slow to exploit this. Lénström and his periodical became in many respects a mouthpiece for Almqvist who directed *Eos* more and more blatantly, to the annoyance of many contemporaries but to the advantage of the present-day literary scholar, who in Lénström's articles, listens to his master's voice. Almqvist's books were reviewed favorably, in several cases at specific directions from the author himself. He well needed all the sunshine that fell upon him, for in this year he finally lost his chances of an academic post, and he (and other people as well) were still discontent with his work as principal of Nya elementarskolan.

CHAPTER 8

Sara Videbeck–*Can It Be Done?*

I *Popular Writings*

IN 1839, too, Almqvist was amazingly productive, but the tone of his writing had now sharpened, and his subjects had grown more controversial.

In the summer he brought out the revised version of the masterpiece of his youth, *Amorina*, provided with a polemic preface, sparkling with wit, satirical and effective. As a foretaste of Almqvist's political writing during the decade to follow, the often quoted lines on the purport of the work resound: "Does this mean that the rapier's sharp point is applied to humanity's most sensitive nerve?"

Two months later appeared the first installments of the ambitiously designed *Saga of Mankind*, defined as *Universal History of the World Combined with Geography*. It is, we might say, a great synthesis of folklore, geography, and history, spiced with Almqvist's lively and daring etymological explanations and with overt references to the political topics of the day. As a whole, it must probably be regarded as a failure; a few passages, however, are highly enjoyable. Especially noteworthy are the original and magnificent "General Reflections on the Formation of Islands on the Earth" or these beautiful lines on the poetry of exotic place-names:

A number of geographical names are often interesting to hear (though the places that they designate may be without any real importance) just because of their sounds and because in our hearts we listen to the sort of melody that floats mysteriously over people and land. This observation is of some importance once it is admitted that the object is not merely to perceive the state of the earth and humankind through the mind and intellect but to realize their intrinsic and higher value, which we cannot do except by means of the wonderful things within us. What leads us to these wonderful things is an ear for music. (*The Saga of Mankind,* p. 96)

Almqvist made similar declarations in connection with "The Palace" (see p. 107 above).

The lively geographical etymology and aesthetics remind us of the little essay, "The Charm of the Map," written much earlier, and reappear in the historical sagas in *Sviavígamál.* Exotic geography had been one of Almqvist's main hobbies ever since he was a boy; he himself, during his long exile, was later to be bombarded by the sound of new place-names.

His longing to write for the common people, manifested in the introduction to "The Significance of Swedish Poverty," found concrete expression in the short sequence of popular works that he published in 1839 and 1840. In the fall of the former year four pieces appeared: *Gustaf Vasa in Dalarne, The Nobility of Work, Grimstahamn's New Settlement,* and *Ryska minnet i Norrköping (Russian Memory in Norrköping).* One year later *The Farm Lease* followed. The two stories, *Grimstahamn's New Settlement* and *The Farm Lease,* remained especially popular, and the former is generally regarded as one of Almqvist's greatest successes.

In *Grimstahamn's New Settlement* the efficient farmhand Johan proposes to the beautiful Katarina and takes over the Grimstahamn croft on the Runsa Estate. The place is dilapidated, but Johan and Katarina toil away on their new holding and gradually improve their position. Johan's mother, Kvast-Lisa, who sells whisks and brooms at the Haymarket in Stockholm, eventually moves in with the young couple and their children and shares their tribulations and happiness until her death.

The Grimstahamn settlers illustrate Almqvist's views on the significance of Swedish poverty, and the short story is an idyll of hard work and happy atmosphere—in a way, inimitably Almqvistian. Yet we note that it is quite unaffected by the thunderclouds that were gathering at that time in relation to *Sara Videbeck* and *The Causes of European Discontent.* The description of Johan's and Katarina's first evening in their new home is justly famous, and so is the description of Kvast-Lisa's

120   CARL JONAS LOVE ALMQVIST

death at the end of the story. These scenes, with their seeming artlessness, are fine examples of the poetry of facts that Almqvist was advocating at that time.

The Farm Lease is also marked by a restrained artistic style and sensible, agreeable message. Beautiful Greta is a sister of Katarina of Grimstahamn and also serves Kvast-Lisa's role as broomhawker at the Haymarket. She is employed as a farm-maid but wants to become her own mistress after a few years. She marries her friend Anders, and they lease cattle belonging to Skansen. Greta is resourceful, inventive, and patient—she demonstrates the virtues extolled in "The Significance of Swedish Poverty." Here—just as in the story of Johan and Katarina—an enterprise is built up, and a goal is reached, and the author describes it all expertly in the voice of the narrator. Greta and Anders take on a larger lease, are successful in all their under-takings, and the story ends with the christening of their first son. In this story too we can speak of "poetry of domesticity," poetry of facts.

The literary manifesto, "On the Poetry of Facts," has already been mentioned. In it Almqvist makes a basic distinction be-tween two sorts of poetry: poetry of facts and poetry of words alone. By way of introduction, poetry and politics are discussed jointly, for both must be reborn. Just as the principal political questions of the day focused on the idea that people should demand "something concrete from the society" ("On the Poetry of Facts," p. 10), the form of poetry must also give way to something concrete: instead of poetry of mere words there must be poetry of facts. "The spirit of our time already is, and is in-creasingly becoming, *a demand for reality*" (p. 9, my italics). Appearance and form have in far too many cases been a poetic mask concealing a lack of substance; but now the final hour of the political and aesthetic masquerade is announced. All subjects are poetic: "Not a single stone on the road is trivial, no cottage is shabby, no situation is unpoetical, whatever it may be, high or low" (p. 15). But it is up to the artists, the poets, to absorb and interpret the various shapes of beauty. The artists are of immense importance; they become, says Almqvist, demonic.

Thus, in "On the Poetry of Facts," both Romantic and Realistic strains are heard at the same time. Almqvist's view of artists as demonic shows him faithful to the Romantic conception of poets as priests and of poetry as a sacrament,[1] but the new view of subject matter and motif, the demand for reality in art and awareness of contemporary problems: these come from the artistic theory of Realism. It is the new trends that are of decisive importance for Almqvist. Those of his later writings which have endured are poetry of facts—whether in fiction or in factual prose.

In the twelfth volume of *The Book of the Wild Rose,* Almqvist was dealing mainly with practical politics; several of these short tracts and speeches are non-fiction, and most had been published in the press before they were included in the *Wild Rose* frame. They will therefore be considered together with Almqvist's journalism.

II   Sara Videbeck—*Subject Matter and Narrative Technique*

Social and political commitment is also characteristic of *Sara Videbeck,* published in December 1839. Its story and thesis have been briefly sketched (p. 21); the book deals with the brave sergeant Albert and Sara Videbeck, the beautiful, energetic daughter of a glazier: their experiences and conversations during a week's journey by steamer and mailcoach from Stockholm to Lidköping persuade them to contract a free marriage. The action extends over a week in summer, and the journey offers an ever changing succession of places and milieux. The steamer and the posting-houses attract different categories of people, from barons and parsons to Dalecarlian women and post-boys. Socially, both Albert and Sara come from a group that would rank somewhere between "better" and "lower" class.

As a work of art, the short novel—or as some prefer, the long short story—is perfect. It was written in a happy mood by a realist delighted with reality.

Sara Videbeck is no fugue, like *Amorina* or *The Queen's Jewel;* it has none of the experimental mixture of genres of the Romantic novel. There is plenty of dialogue in the novel, but no passages arranged in the dramatic dialogue form reminiscent of scenes in a play. The novel dialogue in *Sara Videbeck* is

usually introduced by narrative passages, the narrator's comment or account approaches the point of view of the character
and moves into the latter's direct speech or conversation by
means of introductory formulas. Sixty percent of the text consists
of direct speech—that is to say, the views of the actual characters—whereas the narrator's contribution amounts to only
forty percent.

Both the dialogue and the narrative of Sara Videbeck have
been rightly praised as examples of lively, observant, realistic
writing. The controversial thesis is presented with genial good
humor, and this is also evident from the narrator's own commentary on his writing style and his characters. The narrator
intervenes very conspicuously in his fiction, as he did in the
Romantic fugues. He discourses on the new steamships and
their different classes of passengers, and delights in giving detailed topographic descriptions of Strängnäs and other provincial
towns. This omniscient narrator can, with some indignation,
inform the reader of the sergeant's mistake when at the end of
the novel the latter imagines that his beloved Sara Videbeck
has died (CW, XVI, p. 287).

On several occasions the narrator also takes his time discussing
various problems of narrative technique: "But as a matter of
fact, is it not impossible for a storyteller to follow everything
that happened and to tell everything, little things and big things,
both what was said and what was not said, what happened and
what did not happen?" (CW, XVI, p. 250).

But such illusion-breaking additions are not, as in Amorina,
marked by Romantic humor or Romantic irony; they are rather
pleasant additions in an easygoing conversational tone that does
not seem to take either thesis or illusion very seriously. They
are closer to Dickens than to Laurence Sterne.

III   Characterization and Milieu

The characterization is masterly. The narrator first introduces
Albert, whose appearance is described, whose point of view
is established, and whose monologue is heard. Albert is curious
about a "young female passenger," speculates about her, makes
observations, and draws conclusions from them. In the list

of passengers he finds her name, status, and domicile, he makes advances, talks to her, is rebuffed, tries again, becomes familiar, and through their conversation gets to know more and more about her—her way of life, character traits, and opinions. Thus we come to know Sara via Albert, and of course we learn about Albert at the same time.

The narrator often views and describes the principal characters directly from his own perspective, but the most important characterization is effected indirectly, that is, when the principal figures are to a great extent left to characterize themselves and each other. This is partly a matter of what they say, and partly a question of their way of saying it. (To this may also be added characterization by gestures and acts.)

Sara and Albert both give long accounts of themselves. It is normal that two lovers should tell each other about their past, their fancies, their opinions; they put each other to the test and lay their cards out on the table.

The two characters thus brought face to face are quite unlike. The impatient and enthusiastic Albert is strong in his opening attack, but it is the cool, sensible, and practical Sara who soon takes over, tightens the reins, and determines the way and the goal of their journey together through life.

In the love scenes Almqvist was extremely careful to emphasize Sara's pure disposition and morals—which explains the apparently cool and noncommittal trait in her character—because the subject of the story could easily be judged offensive by readers of his day. What Sara proposes to Albert is simply sexual intercourse between an unmarried man and an unmarried woman, which at that time was against the law in Sweden.[2] But a certain similarity between Sara and other female characters in Almqvist's work can also be detected. There is undeniably something of animal coeleste about Sara Videbeck.

The novel spans a week, and there is a remarkable exactitude in the chronological course of events.

There is also considerable variation in the ratio between the time it takes to narrate events and the time it took for them to occur. The first day (the steamship tour) fills the first four chapters—that is, fifty-five pages, almost half the novel. The period from the third to the sixth day is summed up in less than one page, and within this time Albert and Sara have made up their minds. In the remaining time they discuss thoroughly their future life together.

A good deal has been said about Almqvist's documentary realism: with all the narrator's details about steamboat decks and posting-house rooms, *Sara Videbeck* has become a living picture of the period, ranking almost as a historical document.[3] The topographical surveys and descriptions have the observant, graphic quality as Almqvist's own travel letters. Sometimes the depiction of the scenery is colored by Albert's point of view, becoming romantically personified, as, for instance, in the somewhat erotic description of the sun setting over Kungsör:

> It was evening. In the west the fairy of the sun had already sunk into the arms of the Kungsör meadows, but a dark-red shimmer of purple still lingered in the sky; it was the last garment that the beautiful fairy had cast off before lying down to sleep under the quilt. Thousands of long red-blue streaks radiated from the shimmer, many of them striped the water and some even lay splashed on the objects on board the steamer. (*CW*, XVI, p. 217)

But these Romantic metaphors are exceptions. As a rule, the descriptions of scenery are matter of fact and concrete: travel poetry of facts.

IV *Symbols and Tendency*

Among the striking symbols and symbolism in *Sara Videbeck* we first encounter the steamboat trip. It has been suggested that the narrator's digression on modern steamers and antiquated sailing ships has symbolic significance. Steamers are driven by internal combustion, symbolizing people who follow their own feelings and convictions. The old sailing ships, on the other hand, may be taken to represent the clumsy, unwieldy social institutions that drive people where they do not want to go, causing many a shipwreck.[4]

The marriage controversy, one of the elements of the composition, is introduced in the first chapter when Sara throws a ring into the water: gallant Albert has offered it to her when trying to make her acquaintance. Sara's action soon proves to be a symbolic gesture, and the ring that she flung away is later referred to several times. It turns out—quite conventionally—to be a symbol of the shackles of wedlock.

Time after time Sara is described as an "in-betweener," at first in a social sense, but—as Albert's love for her grows—the term acquires a broader significance (see also p. 128). It becomes associated with the pane of glass which is not seen "and yet definitely separates the Inside of the little human world from the immense Outside. In the pane itself I can see nothing, but through it, nevertheless, I now see the stars in the sky" (p. 227). Albert's musings on the pane of glass and its nature, and his speculations on the heart of glass and the diamond, also perform the functions of leitmotif and symbols. The pane of glass and the heart of glass also symbolize Sara's pure, chaste, and transparent, but at the same time hard and distant nature.

As already mentioned, the basic theme is the marriage debate. But it is not only the form of marriage and the function of the wedding that Almqvist is attacking in his novel. He is also making a topical argument in favor of women's right to work.[5] Almqvist has stressed the absurdity of Sara not being allowed to pursue a trade even though she is quite capable. The novel was published just in time to support reform measures in the Riksdag of 1840 concerning the rights of majority and the trading rights.

As far as love and marriage are concerned, Almqvist argues in favor of a free erotic liaison—with responsibility and true devotion—as a model for the life shared by woman and man.

To keep love alive, the narrator recommends, through Sara, a busy life of travel. The prescription was recommended still more strongly when *Sara Videbeck* was included in the third volume of the imperial octavo edition of 1850. There, in fact, it was immediately preceded by the short sketch, "Why Do You Travel?" in which he eloquently sets forth all the advantages of traveling: on a journey one has time only to show one's better, more pleasant sides: "I must also add that I have the strange advantage when I travel (alone, that is) that almost everybody meets me in divine mood [...] Human beings are like pianos in that they readily return the note that is struck;

and they do not sound false except when they are out of tune"
(*CW*, XVI, p. 164 f.).

People can certainly be out of tune, but seldom when they
are traveling. Consequently we must look upon our whole life
as no more than a journey, and all "dwelling-places should be
regarded as mere *stopping-places*. Can that be done?" That is
how the little essay ends, and *Sara Videbeck*—which ends with
the words "It can be done"—may be regarded as the application
of these ideas to marriage. As far as we can follow Sara's and
Albert's life together, it is lived on a journey, and Albert is
also going to travel a great deal in future, so that they may
benefit fully from the advantages of mobility. In such an alliance
the contracting parties will become happier and better than
couples who are forced, by marriage or common domicile, to
rub elbows all the time.

Here we find a reflection of Almqvist's own matrimonial
situation. It has already been mentioned that his marriage was
not a happy one. A letter to J. A. Hazelius in December 1841
gives further evidence:

My dear Maria is *inwardly* quite angelic in her pure and genuine
kindness, in her fairness and love of truth. But *outwardly* hardly
anybody can be imagined more cumbersome or difficult for a man
who must occupy himself with what he ought to do and would
like to do. No shoe is mended, no chair is put in its right place, no
turnip is bought without my having to give my opinion five or ten
times over and usually then attending to the matter myself. People
do not know this and nobody will believe it. Many people think that
I have been sitting all by myself, a free and happy dreamer, giving
myself up to all sorts of blissful thoughts. Since you once broached
the subject, Janne, I tell you that I have *suffered* and am still
suffering. (*Letters*, p. 162)

But in spite of everything, he still loves Maria sincerely, Almqvist says, especially in moments of loneliness and when he is
away from home. There is in Maria's personality a very strange
combination—"at the same time heaven and slovenly chaos"—
which makes her difficult to live with.

It is obvious that the discrepancy between husband and wife
as to temperament and intellectual level was never to be re-

solved. But outbursts like the above-quoted example are rare, and in spite of his negative comments on wedding and marriage, Almqvist accepted his own ill-matched marriage, perhaps for practical reasons, perhaps because, in his own way, he always retained his tender feelings toward his wife. During the longest separation of all, his years of exile in America, an unaffected and deep tenderness marks his letters to Maria.

In the appendix to *Sara Videbeck* Almqvist denies that it is a tendentious novel and tries to explain what is meant by "tendency." Almqvist definitely repudiates any mixing of "doctrinaire, agitatorial, or scientific literature with fiction. Both parties—on the one hand, the message, the explanation, the discussion, and on the other, the fiction—will lose through an ill-matched union."[6] Almqvist maintains that only such theoretical arguments as belong organically to the fiction and are justified by it, should be accepted. If not,

the lessons, however good they may be in themselves, have nevertheless been unartistically inserted into the piece and constitute what in a pejorative sense may be termed *creatures of tendency*. They stand there so to speak on account of the author or rather of the doctrines as such; which is out of place because such things belong to science, not to art. (*CW*, XVI, p. 298)

Thus Almqvist deprecates the "bad," inartistic tendentious literature of his time, with its loosely attached ideas imperfectly integrated into the fiction. That "good" thesis novels may exist is a fact that Almqvist seems to ignore; obviously we cannot speak of a tendency when, for instance, Sara is speaking. Her arguments are "in full accordance with her character and are fully justified by the situation or the incident, for she has every reason and motive to utter them when she does so [...] the lessons are not there for their own sake or for the sake of the narrator" (*CW*, XVI, p. 298).

These explanations show Almqvist as an extremely clever theorist of narrative technique.

However, we might then well ask whether the novel fulfills Almqvist's own requirements. His characterization of Sara provides the answer. One thing is obvious: If Almqvist had meant

Sara to be a typical glazier's daughter in the 1830s, the opinions that she expresses would certainly have seemed inappropriate in her mouth. On the contrary, Almqvist has emphasized that Sara is *not* typical. On the contrary, he constantly stresses what is unique, uncommon about her. From the very beginning Sara appears to Albert as an in-betweener:

A mademoiselle? Yes, in a way. A burgher's daughter, though of the lowest burgher class. An attractive and strange in-betweener! Not a country girl, certainly not a peasant girl—but not quite better class either. How should such a person be regarded? What should she be called? There is something impenetrable about this inter-mediate sort. (*CW*, XVI, p. 177)

Albert's speculations about Sara's social status are continued on another level, as if she is quite unfathomable to him. Thus, it seems perfectly consistent for her to have unusual opinions, all the more so as Almqvist motivates them by her personal experiences, particularly her parents' unhappy marriage. It must also be said that the conversations about marriage are introduced quite naturally: the topic is an obvious one for two persons falling in love with each other.

The original version of *Sara Videbeck* was provided with a preface which in 1850 was included in the appendix. In the preface the author is—rightly—convinced that he has a future before him:

It is said that a fine veil hangs before the future of Europe pre-venting us seeing distinctly the figures that beckon to us behind it. I think so, too. The veil is not quite transparent, in some places its beautiful drapery hangs in somewhat thicker folds than in others making it less easy to see through it. [. . .] Nobody can or should know the individual fate that awaits us in the future; but the general fate, . . . the general direction . . . is clearly indicated to us. (*CW*, XVI, p. 292)

V *The* Sara Videbeck *Controversy*

Not even Almqvist's dialectics could conceal the fact that *Sara Videbeck* is a novel with a tendency or thesis. Both his contemporaries and posterity concur in this. But agreement ends there; in our day many consider the argument natural and justified but most of his contemporaries regarded it as subversive and disruptive. Even Almqvist's friends and groups favorably disposed toward him reacted with restraint, to say the least; his adversaries became very vocal.

Atterbom denounced *Sara Videbeck*, and even the faithful and broad-minded J. A. Hazelius disapproved of it. In a letter a few years later Hazelius emphasized the fateful consequences that the publication had for the author:

If you had confined yourself to publishing only the novel—or, to publishing several in the same spirit—and letting it work on its own, then nothing much would have happened. But you did not only publish it with a *preface* that did *not originally* belong to the novel, and which was *an essay* on the subject, but you figured polemically in the newspapers and maintained that formal marriage was dispensable, you attacked the marriages of today in a way that was interpreted to be directed against *marriage in itself*; you spoke of a new *system* that had been introduced by the It-can-be-done-book [*Sara Videbeck*] etc., all of which I disapprove of since your purpose was to further your idea by means not of a treatise but of a novel. This was what attracted a suspicious attention to your *person* which the novelist would never have attracted, at least not to the same extent. (*CW*, XVI, p. xxxii)

In a letter to Atterbom, Almqvist again stressed the sincerity of his intentions with *Sara Videbeck*:

don't you believe what many others imagine about me, namely that I am now writing *hastily* and consequently *superficially* a lot of things without thinking. You may rest assured that for twenty years at least, in moments of deep solitude, I have reflected upon the ideas behind what I am now writing. People find that several things are obvious and therefore they approve of them; other parts will be understood later. What not even my most fanatical enemies can deny is that I am working for higher purposes than the mere promotion or advancement of my own person, literary fame, etc., for in that case I would have adapted my production to what was demanded (and I have clearly proved that I *can* write popular things when I want to) instead of adapting them to what I believe to be true, right, and beautiful, as I have done. That *Sara Videbeck* would rouse almost all opinions against it was something I knew quite well; in its basic idea it is far ahead of our time; and what one does not want to see or cannot see now, namely that it stands *for* Morality and *against* Immorality, will some day be seen and admitted. (*Letters*, p. 147 f.)

Sara Videbeck attracted great attention, and as early as March 1840, Fredrika Bremer compared it (in a letter to Malla Silfverstolpe) to a comet whose tail was growing longer and longer. The tail consisted not only of newspaper articles, but also of several writings in their turn prompted by these. With malicious logic, the Swedo-Finnish author, J. V. Snellman, developed the sequel to Albert's and Sara's liaison: *Det går an, en tafla, fortsättning* (*It Can Be Done, a Picture, Continued*), a withering perspective which enraged Almqvist. August Blanche contributed with another sequel of a somewhat burlesque character entitled *Sara Widebeck. En tafla ur lifvet* (*Sara Widebeck. A Picture from Life*). From his old Uppsala friends came at least two pamphlets: Malla Silfverstolpe's *Månne det går an?* (*Can It Really Be Done?*), meant to be serious but according to Almqvist harmless, and Palmblad's *Törnrosens bok. Nemligen den äkta och veritabla, utgifven icke af Richard Furumo utan Hofmarskalken Hugo Löwenstjerna sjelf* (*The Book of the Wild Rose. Namely the Genuine and True Version. Published Not by Richard Furumo but by the Court Chamberlain Hugo Löwenstjerna Himself*).

The Sara Videbeck controversy—one of the few notable literary quarrels in the history of Swedish letters—came to have an injurious effect on the author's future.

CHAPTER 9

Old Wild Rose Writings and a New Novelistic Style

I   *New* Wild-Rose *Volumes*

IN December 1839, *The Book of the Wild Rose* was published in another series and another format; it comprised the first part of the splendid imperial octavo edition. From among its contents we have already mentioned "The Tears of Beauty," "Ormus and Ariman," and "The Song of the Moon"; it also includes the beautiful drama, *Ferrando Bruno*, which in accordance with the ideas put forward in *Murnis* is enacted in the land of ghosts. *Svangrottan på Ipsara* (*The Swan Cave of Ipsara*), a drama in classical style, also dates from this period.

In this volume we also find the two theological dramas, *Isidoros of Tadmor* and *Marjam*, written in about the middle of the 1830s. Both are based on material from early Christian times, and express Almqvist's longing for the simple doctrines of primitive Christianity. In *Marjam* there appears a stranger who has no name but who is clearly meant to be St. Paul. This character expresses himself in a confused and pretentious manner, and his arguments are in striking contrast to the teaching of the other apostle, St. John, whose doctrine is nearer to that of Christ. This is an early appearance of a theme which was to recur frequently in Almqvist's later creative writing and journalism. It is the view that genuine Christianity quickly petrified into dogma as the result of intrusive explanations and interpretations. In the writings of David Friedrich Strauss and others, Almqvist had been able to study the radical theology that emanates from the lines of *Marjam*.

Among the varied works in the first volume of the imperial octavo edition is also a short story, or rather an anecdote in the

131

form of a letter, "From Leonard," to the following effect: in despair a lover writes to a friend about a horrible experience: he has just visited his beloved at the hospital for venereal diseases. The woman has been unfaithful to him but loves him nevertheless; he himself loves her, but his mind reels before this specimen of female psychology and the erotic complexes that are suggested. Magnus von Platen has rightly remarked that this little study is among the strangest things that Almqvist ever wrote.[1] His contemporaries' opinion of the story is exemplified by the delicate commentary of Almqvist's admirer, Topelius, who noted that often "two leaves of the imperial Wild Rose were glued together before people risked leaving the book in the hands of young ladies."[2]

Arthurs jakt ("Arthur's Hunt"), a splendid verse tale echoing with the merry hunting horns of the Middle Ages and Sir Walter Scott, dates from the middle of the 1830s, as does the charming little verse epic, "Schems-el-Nihar," set in an exotic Abyssinia complete with savage lions and a Nubian princess (hastily christianized in the end).

In the spring of 1840 Almqvist took a leave of absence from his school principalship, and in July he started his journey to France and England which was to last more than six months. Immediately before leaving, he turned in the manuscript of the thirteenth part of *The Book of the Wild Rose*, containing the superb short story, "*Målaren*" ("The Painter") and "The Clergyman's Situation," reflections of topical interest. "The Painter" deals with a young man who has been lax and extravagant, but, after an illness, he is taught by an itinerant decorator how to paint and work, and to become a useful citizen. In many respects the painter seems to be a self-portrait of Almqvist, who has now turned to reality and the world and wants to become a popular reformer.[3]

II   Amalia Hillner *and* Gabrièle Mimanso

Earlier that summer Almqvist had published the novel, *Amalia Hillner*. The story follows:

A. E. Hillner, a respected estate owner, becomes insolvent—partly through business transactions with a certain Baron Ekensparre—and pretends to be dead and secretly goes abroad. Shortly afterward his wife, who believes he is dead, gives birth to a daughter named Amalia. While he is abroad, Hillner changes his identity and becomes Baron Migneul. Believing his wife to be dead, he marries Eugénie, widow of Baron Ekensparre, and returns to Sweden and settles down on the Ekensparre estate of Gräseholm. By Eugénie he has a daughter, Constance; his wife's stepsons, Oscar and Malcolm Ekensparre, are also members of the family.

When the novel begins, Amalia Hillner has just been taken on as a governess at Gräseholm, under the name of Lenoir. At the same time, Oscar is exploring the possibility of bringing an action against Migneul for the inheritance. Oscar soon finds out that Migneul and Hillner are the same person, and Migneul learns that his first wife is alive and that, in the event of a lawsuit, he runs the risk of being prosecuted for bigamy. In the meantime, Oscar and Amalia have fallen in love with each other. Father and daughter recognize one another, and an amicable arrangement is arrived at between Oscar, Migneul, and Amalia.

Baroness Eugénie conveniently dies, and under the reassumed name of Hillner, Migneul can be reunited with his first wife. Amalia marries Oscar.

The bigamy motif is an essential part of the novel; in a letter to Sturzen-Becker, Almqvist pointed out that the main theme of this novel is

the demonstration of the psychological fact that a person can love several persons simultaneously (as Hillner or Migneul loves both Eugénie and Beat-Sofie) and do so in a heavenly, warm, pure way. (This is generally regarded as impossible, and polygamous love is thought to exist only in an impure sense.) To *prove* this as a theoretical thesis would not be necessary, especially as nobody would believe in that sort of evidence; but if the description of the characters of the three persons mentioned above is true, which I do not think anybody can deny, then the fact in question is practically *shown* in my little novel. (*Letters*, p. 156)

And in *Den sansade kritiken* (*Sober Criticism*), *Amalia Hillner* is held up as "an important link added to the chain of thought of *Sara Videbeck* itself" (*CW*, XV, p. 422).

In the novel, however, the conflict is not carried to extremes. Hillner believes himself to be a widower when he marries Eugénie, and she dies before learning of his first wife's existence.

During his stay in France, Almqvist also gathered material for his next great novel, *Gabrièle Mimanso*, subtitled *The Last Attempt to Murder King Louis Philippe of France, in the Fall of 1840*, which was published in 1841–42.

The subtitle gives an idea of the main plot and establishes the time and place of the novel. This plot is:

The young nobleman, Constantin de Montmorency of Normandy, comes to Paris and is attracted by a mysterious beauty, dressed in black, Gabrièle Mimanso. Gabrièle, who has both French and Arabian blood in her veins, is the niece of the Arab prince Abdel-Keder. She believes that her father has been murdered by order of Louis Philippe and is firmly resolved to take revenge on the King. But Louis Philippe is innocent; it transpires that Gabrièle has become involved in the conspiracy of a secret revolutionary society, the Eagle Club, led by Father Ambrose Hyacinthe alias Count de Ruonville. The Eagle Club is trying to channel the revolutionary fervor of artisans and workmen into a violent riot in order to overthrow the King and bring Ruonville to power with absolute rule over France. It is Ruonville who has had Gabrièle's father murdered and who, in Gabrièle, has now found a willing tool for his plans to kill the King in the course of the riot.

However, Ruonville is unmasked by Montmorency, who escapes with Gabrièle. Ruonville makes a counter-move and kidnaps Gabrièle, who again runs away to save the King, and meets with exciting adventures in the street fighting. In one section Almqvist himself appears incidentally in the colony of Swedish artists under the name of Cilalma. Through an intricate course of events, the principal characters are captured and by turns set free. The whole affair is further complicated by the fact that, at the end of Part II, Montmorency becomes convinced that Gabrièle loves Ruonville. He breaks with her for a time and fights a duel with Ruonville. In the last part Montmorency and Gabrièle, now reunited, are taken to North Africa for new adventures—the description of the crossing during a storm is excellent—where among other things a lion hunt adds to the suspense. A message arrives that Ruonville has gone insane and that he has taken his own life. Montmorency and Gabrièle marry.

In a preface in the form of a letter, the author meditates on poetry and politics, on the Middle Ages and the present time. He contrasts the fine nuances in modern descriptions of mental conditions with the lack of nuances in the Middle Ages, and shows how the family novel has assumed the role of the epic.

The studied intrigue of the novel suggests the influence of trivial literature, and Almqvist's interest in Kotzebue, Lafontaine, and Spiess has been established. Almqvist's liking for these horror-filled, sentimental "lending library novels," which dates back to his childhood, found a new direction when the serial novel took up the romanticism and the primitive naturalism of older times in the form of adventures and social message. In Paris it was quite natural for Almqvist to find an influence in the kind of literature whose chief exponents were Eugène Sue and Dumas. But there are other French writers whom Almqvist may also have taken as models. He was quite familiar with the works of both Victor Hugo and Balzac. Werin has pointed out that the beginning of *Gabrièle Mimanso,* in which the principal character is strolling in the streets of Paris on the trail of an attractive young lady, is very reminiscent of Balzac's *Histoire des treize,* which in fact had been published in an abridged Swedish translation in 1834. Father Hyacinthe and the Eagle Club also have their counterparts in Ferragus and l'Ordre des Dévorants in Balzac's novel.[4]

Werin has also shown that *Gabrièle Mimanso* has several elements in common with *The Queen's Jewel.* In both novels there is a conspiracy to murder the king of the country. Louis Philippe has an amulet that can be regarded as the counterpart of the jewel in the earlier work. Moreover, certain familiar features are to be found in Gabrièle and Tintomara; they both behave like pure, unconscious children of nature, and both have something about them that is more "fairy-like than human."[5]

Almqvist's own travel impressions and political interests color the novel to a great extent. Louis Blanc himself appears in the book and defines what seems to be Almqvist's political stance: he is the friend of the people and the workers but warns against armed rebellion. The enemies of the people will nevertheless "*fall through their own deeds.* For we shall only meet them with the law, the truth, and reason" (*CW*, XXIV, p. 108).

Gabrièle Mimanso got a mixed reception; at best the critics found the beginning promising but there was little enthusiasm for the later parts.

III   Three Ladies in Småland

Almqvist's next great novel, *Tre fruar i Småland* (*Three Ladies in Småland*), followed in 1842–43 and its first part was published at the same time as the last part of *Gabrièle Mimanso*. Both the introduction and the ending fit well into the Wild Rose frame. Its contents are a mixture of message, idyll, and picaresque stories.

The admirable private tutor Alexander Medenberg is engaged by the von Mekeroth family who own the Aronsfors factory. He deservedly wins the complete confidence of everyone in the family. When Nickolson, the manager of the factory, absconds with all the money in his charge, leaving the accounts in a deplorable mess, Medenberg is commissioned to clear the situation up. He begins with current account books, discovers a connection between Nickolson and Count Zeyton of the neighboring estate of Karmansbol (Nickolson is in fact the count's illegitimate son), and intervenes energetically. The father and son maintain a dangerous association with a great band of robbers infesting Småland. Medenberg's prospective brother-in-law, the student Göran Edling, and Edling's bold and ready-witted servant, Jeppe Jonsson (with some assistance from other people), overcome the dangerous robbers, who are captured; Count Zeyton dies and Nickolson is converted.

Zeyton's wife, Countess Celestine, and Aurora, wife of Captain von Mekeroth, and Ebba, wife of Abelcrona, Marshall of the Court, have been left widows before the end of the novel. These beautiful and philanthropic women are the three ladies in Småland who have given the novel its name. Under Medenberg's wise guidance, these women form an association for the rehabilitation of criminals, and start a colony for converted robbers who are given remedial treatment in the backwoods of Småland in order to help them mend their ways.

Thus, Almqvist takes up those ideas he had presented previously in his essay, "On the Treatment of Criminals," and in *Amorina.*

Three Ladies in Småland is undoubtedly the best of the novels Almqvist wrote in the '40s. It is at times very exciting and has some brilliant settings. Moreover, it is of great interest as "the last literary work in which Almqvist occupied himself extensively with his ideas of social and religious reform. Here he subjected them to a thorough general review."[6]

In the *Wild Rose* introduction, the novel is said to have been written by Richard Furumo, who—like Almqvist, has settled temporarily at Jönköping. Here the novel is called "the little caprice frome the southern shore of Lake Vätter, this *Play of the Junecoping Ministrel.*" This makes reference to one of Almqvist's favorite models, Sir Walter Scott, and later in the novel his master is mentioned by name. In the introduction, the Hunting Seat circle also discuss various possible titles for the novel, such as "Småland's Last War" or "The Värnamo Robber Band," names that are reminiscent of Walter Scott's book titles.

In the conclusion, which bears the title "Academic Thoughts," the listeners at the Hunting Seat comment on the novel and discuss such features as philanthropy and pietism, etymology, the mystery of crime, and the treatment of criminals.

Three Ladies in Småland also failed to arouse any great enthusiasm among the critics, and Almqvist himself took the precaution of including a study of the novel in his long series of newspaper articles *"De stora frågorna om paragraf-moral och själsmoral"* ("The Great Questions of Paragraph Morals and Emotional Morals") in *Aftonbladet,* December 1843–January 1844. Here Almqvist, discussing his own novel and also works by Fredrika Bremer and Sophie von Knorring, emphasizes that the author of *Three Ladies in Småland,* unlike the two other writers, takes up a position definitely in favor of more humane treatment of criminals. After stressing the social message of his work in this vigorous manner, Almqvist also hastened to attract more superficial readers: around this message "a great number of the most varied adventures are presented, just like the serpents around a straight staff of Mercury or, better still, like the vines round a thyrsus."

IV   The Emerald Bride *and* Sister and Brother

In the summer of 1845 Almqvist published the novel, *Smaragd-bruden* (*The Emerald Bride*), subtitled "The Effects of a Great Nordic Heritage." This is a summary of its contents:

The noble-minded but impoverished young man Gustaf Carl Mannerskog is taking a walk in Djurgården in Stockholm, when he is attracted by a beautiful unknown girl: he follows her. At the inn, Blå Porten, he finds an address and the remnants of a letter which he believes the beautiful girl has left by mistake. The letter gives strange directions as to how to find a certain key and also a casket containing important objects. Mannerskog makes up his mind to follow the instructions, and in so doing becomes involved in an adventurous plot. He manages to outwit some unknown scoundrels and to gain possession of a brass key that fits a casket hidden in Katarina churchyard. There Mannerskog is locked up but is rescued from his pursuers by a benevolent ghost. In a striking dream scene that night, Mannerskog also meets King Christian II ("the Tyrant") and the ninety-four victims of the Stockholm massacre of 1520.

The mysterious casket contains an account of the rich Jonas Lambert's life, success, and millions and also an indication as to the whereabouts of Lambert's last will. The casket also contains 100,000 riksdollars in cash. Mannerskog, who is an honest man, wants to turn the casket over to the unknown beauty whom he believes to be its rightful owner, and he succeeds in identifying her as one of two German ladies. However, they have left Sweden. Mannerskog goes to Hamburg and manages to find the women, who tell him more about the Lambert millions that beautiful Isabella is to inherit. After several complications with villainous bankers and presumptive co-heirs, Mannerskog at last wins both Isabella (The Emerald Bride) and the millions.

As we will recall, Almqvist attached great importance to the art of finishing pieces. He hardly does so in this novel, at the end of which the narrator addresses himself to the reader saying that what happened to the personages afterward is none of his business. Instead he makes the following suggestion:

"And so, dear reader, we will stop here. And since you have done me the favor of passing over with me so many misprints and other mistakes which we will discuss frankly when we are alone, then let me treat you to a glass or two of honest soda water at Carlmarken's on parting! Would you like some fruit syrup with it?" (*CW*, XXVIII, p. 476)

The reader is treated to soda water, but he is no longer asked to contribute to the story.

The subject of Almqvist's novel is authentic insofar as the disputes about the Lambert inheritance did take place. In January 1845, particularly, they were much in the news; among other actions, a direct appeal was made in the matter to the Government.

Thus authentic material was at hand for Almqvist, and scholars have also claimed associations with Eugène Sue's novels *The Wandering Jew* and *The Mysteries of Paris*.[7] The *Wandering Jew* includes discussion of an enormous inheritance, and the noble-minded central figure in *The Mysteries of Paris* has inexhaustible riches at his disposal. Mention may also be made of Dumas's Count of Montechristo, who generally carried a few millions on him as pocket money. Isabella's mother undoubtedly has something of the same habit:

"'Just now we are not in need of anything,' she answered gracefully, half rising to say good-bye. 'However, there may be a few trifles we ought to settle in passing,' she concluded, 'so you might send me eight million banco, or ten, if you feel like it'" (*CW*, XXVIII, p. 309).

As far as the author of the novel is concerned personally, it is tempting to talk of fantasy speculation in this regard. In the novel, the Lambert inheritance amounts to more than 500 million in cash, and, as has often been said, it is possible that Almqvist—whose financial position was wretched—sustained himself by playing with fictitious golden millions.

At times the narrator tears himself away from capitalist felicity and casts a critical eye on contemporary and social problems. In the course of the novel he attacks pietism, advocates women's right to education and culture, and gives a brief but brutal picture of prostitution in Hamburg.

For the most part the novel was unfavorably reviewed; one reviewer called *The Emerald Bride* "certainly the most worthless of Mr. Almqvist's works." Almqvist had to come to the defense of the novel with an (unsigned) review in *Jönköpings-bladet* of December 30, 1845. In this newspaper article he refers to Sue and Sue's works but curiously enough maintains that *The Emerald Bride* was meant to be a parody of Sue's writings.

The novel, *Syster och bror* (*Sister and Brother*), with the provocative subtitle "One of Stockholm's Secrets," was published in May 1847. In the introductory chapters of this book Almqvist returned to the 1790s, the period that he depicted so charmingly in *The Queen's Jewel.*

The foundlings Jacob and Helena are taken care of, first by a philanthropic middle-class woman and later by a count and countess who have no biological children. The foundlings grow up and fall in love with each other but do not know whether or not they are brother and sister. It is now the intent of the two lovers to establish the identity of their true parents in order to ascertain whether their love is incestuous.

Complications of all sorts stand in the way of their quest for their unknown parents and take the couple on journeys to Denmark and finally to Italy, where definite proof is established, and the two young people are married.

Almqvist has combined two extremely popular motifs: the foundling motif and the motif of love between brother and sister. In so doing he has, as Olle Holmberg has said, "also been able to satisy great expectations of an intricate and sentimental intrigue."[8] Almqvist might have found models in Captain Marryat and Eugène Sue—not to mention Dickens's *Oliver Twist* —as far as the foundling motif was concerned. As to the motif of love between brother and sister, there are close similarities with Lafontaine's *Brother and Sister, or Repentance and Reconciliation,* which was translated into Swedish in 1821.[9] As is usual in Almqvist's novels, the topographical descriptions—in this case of Stockholm and Copenhagen—are detailed and masterly.

A count interested in literature also figures in the novel, and in this connection the author presents aspects of the literary scene in Sweden around about 1810, when the "New Romantics" or "Phosphorists" made their appearance.

Sister and Brother got a mixed reception; in this case, too, Almqvist helped it along with a review of his own, published in *Aftonbladet* on August 10, 1847. The reviewer in *Post-*

Tidningen had taken offense at the behavior of one of the personages in the novel, which with some justifications he found objectionable. But Almqvist says that this can never be "a reason for attacking the novel in question which has only narrated the events without in any way expressing approval of them. Baron Adolf Emil is described pitilessly as a scoundrel in every case where he behaves like one." In this connection Almqvist makes the following fundamental observation which is eminently reasonable:

> Where real history is concerned, there are, as everyone knows, a large number of facts which by their very nature and their psychological character are highly interesting, strange, and likely to cast some light on the human mind and the most secret recesses of the heart; but no one has alleged that all these things are consequently fine and excellent. The same applies to art, where the portrayal is faithful. But do people maintain on that account that no such things must be related? Is nothing except what is good in actual history or in fiction worth relating and describing? Such a gross absurdity has never yet been proclaimed. If it were accepted, neither history nor fiction would exist, and humankind, with its thousand varieties of good and evil, could not be explained, expounded or explored. What can very justifiably be demanded on the part of true morality is, however, that the more or less evil things described should not be defended in the narrative but presented for what they are. (*AB*, August 10, 1847)

V The Ekolsund Counts

In 1847 Almqvist also published the novel, *Herrarne på Ekolsund* (*The Ekolsund Counts*). The subtitle, *A Novel from the Middle of the Last Century*, fixes the period, and later in the text the year is specified as 1743. The counts Robert, Claes, Tage, and Åke Thott are brothers, and each of them wants to gain possession of Ekolsund Castle. This castle which previously belonged to the Thott family but was confiscated by the Crown as part of Charles XI's reduction, had been given by King Fredrik to his former mistress, Countess Hedvig Taube.

Each of the Thott brothers has an artful plan: by magic (an enchanted portrait) Robert tries to make Hedvig cede him the estate; Claes is engaged to Hedvig's confidante, the beautiful

Marie Susanne, and claims that he has obtained a promise that he will be the countess's heir; Tage becomes engaged to the daughter of the villainous administrator of Ekolsund; Åke is going to marry a rich widow so as to have some money behind him and be able to claim the castle back from the Crown.

The different plans are developed, combined, and combated in ingenious ways; the suspense increases when the brothers get in touch, by various means, with a powerful league of thieves and counterfeiters which has a great deal of influence and good connections with the police, even access to high society. The principal characters are involved in fights; especially noteworthy is a magnificant skirmish at Kungshatt, in which the combatants include a band of robber-Amazons who engage in throwing lassos. At a hunt the jovial King Fredrik meets the Thott brothers with their female partners and reveals that he knows all about their plans.

However, the intrigues continue; Åke is eventually murdered and the news spreads that the countess is slowly being poisoned. Finally, the King brings matters to a head and decides that Ekolsund shall be an entailed estate held in trust by his eldest son by Hedvig Taube. The surviving Thott brothers are compensated in various ways.

In his last novels Almqvist reverts to the historical genre. Just as *Sister and Brother* has a time-based connection with *The Queen's Jewel,* so *The Ekolsund Counts* and *Amorina* share a setting in the Age of Freedom. The description of the scenery is sharp and vivid; Almqvist never tires of describing his beloved Stockholm and its surroundings. On the other hand, in this novel he shows hardly any real interest in political or social questions.

The Ekolsund Counts was received coolly by the reviewers. Young S. A. Hedlund was particularly severe in his cutting review in *Dagligt Allehanda* on December 10, 1847. Almqvist replied at great length in the same paper on January 4, 1848.

S. A. Hedlund discussed the improbability of the events and the milieu and says that, "since Lafontaine's and Baron von Bilderbeck's times," he had not read anything so affected or unnatural. He found the novel boring and concluded:

After reading it one has a feeling of emptiness, and more than that, of sadness and distress, at the recollection of what this author was once to us and at the thought of what he *could* be. Where are the beautiful pictures of "The Chapel," "Schems-el-nihar," "The Painter," etc., etc., that Almqvist used to bring before our eyes? Have they faded, have they vanished? Will they never come back? (*DA,* December 10, 1847)

In his long reply Almqvist attacked Hedlund, "whose criticism consists in stating that what I am writing does not contain what Mr. Hedlund had expected from me" (*DA,* January 4, 1848). The remainder of Almqvist's defense was of a rather sophistic quality and hardly touches on the problems raised by Hedlund.

The Ekolsund Counts was Almqvist's last novel. It was followed by a reprint of *Murnis* and *Sara Videbeck* in the third volume of the imperial octavo edition of 1850.

CHAPTER 10

Journalism and Politics

I *Almqvist the Journalist*

GENERALLY speaking, Almqvist's journalism is still unexplored territory. Werin and Westman Berg have mapped out certain important areas, and Ruben G:son Berg has rendered most valuable service in establishing authorship.[1] But a sound basis for a comprehensive view of Almqvist's work as a journalist is still lacking, as we have no scholarly collected edition of his newspaper articles, not even a complete list of his journalistic contributions.

Almquistiana, the bibliography, following a list drawn up by Almqvist himself and intended for the *Dictionary of Biography*, also includes a collection of articles which was probably compiled by Almqvist, and mentions 242 articles or series of articles. Even without checking all the newspapers of immediate interest, Ruben G:son Berg and other scholars have added about 250 articles. At a rough estimate there would seem to exist between 500 and 600 articles from Almqvist's hand.

Almqvist also published some of this material in book form as, for instance, the education articles in *Om svenska uppfostringsväsendet* (*On the Swedish Educational System*, 1840) which is a critical investigation of Swedish schools and universities. He published aesthetic, theological, and political articles in *Monography* and political articles in *The Causes of European Discontent*, to which reference will be made later. "On the Poetry of Facts" was published in article form before being reprinted in *Monography*; and several contributions to *The Book of the Wild Rose*, such as "*Vad är penningen?*" ("What is Money?") or "Poetry and Politics" first appeared in the daily press.[2]

The subjects treated in Almqvist's journalistic writings fall

144

roughly into four groups: a) education, b) theology, c) political and social problems, and d) aesthetics.

It is evident that Almqvist's professional and personal interests formed a happy combination and determined his choice of subjects. That Almqvist, as principal of an educational establishment and author of textbooks, should cover education questions in *Aftonbladet* is not remarkable; school and university problems were always in the news, and it was with the long series of articles, "On the Swedish Educational System," that Almqvist made his brilliant début as a contributor to *Aftonbladet*. Ordained in 1837, Almqvist enjoyed writing on theological questions in the press; from the very beginning he was a liberal, and after his controversies with the Cathedral Chapter of Uppsala, he put forth more and more radical views. As a man of letters he was a frequent critic and debater of æsthetic and literary questions. And finally, in the 1840s, his challenging and committed articles on political and social questions of the day were perhaps his most important writings during this period.

A variety of articles from different years will now be examined.

II *Pedagogic and Theological Articles*

In the first article of his series, "On the Swedish Educational System," Almqvist discussed fundamental questions. He pointed out that the progress of humankind toward improvement and freedom rested on two fundamental pillars: *the art of printing* and *universal education*. The former was "the basis and has been the precondition of the latter." But universal education was nevertheless "the real goal without which the former would lose its historical importance" (*AB,* January 5, 1839).

The gift bestowed by the art of printing was free speech, and that was necessarily the basis of the universal education which led up to religious and political reform. Its tools had been "two kinds of literature, for which the pious books and newspapers have constituted and still constitute not the sole or exclusive but the chief levers and means of distribution" (*AB,* January 5, 1839). To this Almqvist added the need for a third reform, "that of *family life* and individual *morals,* perhaps more

important than the previous two, perhaps the goal of both of
them" (*Ibid.*).

The literature that was to bring about this reform was
"Poetical Writing," mainly in the novel and the drama, and
Almqvist declared:

Poetry can be a highly important means of general education if it
is composed in the right way and is employed with true artistry.
A *description of human beings* as they really are and at all stages
of life: full *justice* done to all conditions, by showing what they
essentially are or may be according to circumstance: a *picture* of all
kinds of scenery, according to the different character of countries
and climates: that is what would interest us in Poetry. Besides
entertaining people thoroughly and infinitely, which would probably
be its main purpose, an artistic description of this kind would not
bring the profit of true *instruction* any the less because it gave us
an insight into a thousand mysterious facts which it always is and
remains impossible for Science to explain clearly but which Art can
make us perceive and understand in its own way. (*Ibid.*)

These suggestions, I think, are not far from Balzac's conception
of literature, humanity, and society, as expressed in the preface
to *La Comédie humaine*.

After his circumstantial reflections, Almqvist once again
spoke in favor of individual human beings who were "so un-
kind as not to be idle abstractions but living persons," and
then passed on to concrete problems affecting the organization
of school and university.

In the spring of 1842 Almqvist wrote several series of articles
on theological subjects of topical interest. The most important
was "Strauss, evangelierna och mamsell Bremer" ("Strauss, the
Gospels, and Miss Bremer"), in which he discussed the radical
German theologian D. F. Strauss, who had been the target of
a pamphlet by Fredrika Bremer. Almqvist took up Fredrika
Bremer's pretentious criticism of Strauss and stated that it had
four qualities:

a peculiarity, a weakness, an eccentricity, and one merit. The
Peculiarity consists in the fact that the author has set herself up
as a violent adversary of Strauss, but that, during the subsequent

treatment of the subject, she has shown that her own views, if she really has any, coincide with those of Strauss, except for very minor differences in expression. The *Weakness* lies in the fact that in this controversy she has not brought up any new argument though she has started with such confidence in her weapons. The *Eccentricity* seems to show itself in her desire to use biblical quotations in archaic language as though greater holiness or better Christianity were concealed in discarded Swedish dative and accusative forms than in the endings used today. The *Merit*, however, is that the whole work reflects an extremely kind heart. (*AB*, February 28, 1842)

After this introductory characterization of Fredrika Bremer, Almqvist passed on to the theological problems, which he discussed clearly and pedagogically and with excellent semantic distinctions. On each point he presented Strauss's opinion and analyzed Miss Bremer's attitude. He arrived at the conclusion that she concurred with Strauss on each point, that is to say, she "agrees on the main direction but is wrong on the application and definitions" (*AB*, March 10, 1842).

"Strauss, the Gospels, and Miss Bremer" was an excellent, inventive and well-written series of articles which brought politico-social and æsthetic views to bear on the theological subject matter. It was one of Almqvist's most striking achievements in the field of journalism.

These articles were followed by a polemic series in reply to criticism leveled against Almqvist in the conservative newspaper, *Svenska Biet* (*The Swedish Bee*). In "*Biets högsta politik*" ("The Highest Politics of the Bee," *AB*, April 1, 1842) Almqvist tackled the question of the clergy—which he had discussed several times before.

There were, Almqvist said, *two* kinds of clergy, so essentially different that it was important to distinguish clearly between them. The *lower clergy*, from schoolmasters and curates to vicars, constituted *one* kind. They were *the true clergy*,

they exist for the sake of Christianity, are close to the people, work for the people's welfare, education, consolation and assistance, or would and could at least do all that, if they were not prevented from doing so by interference from higher quarters.

148   CARL JONAS LOVE ALMQVIST

It is this kind of clergy which in our day aims at bringing
things nearer to the people, for the sake of whom they exist; the
theology of these ministers conforms to the words of Christ.

The other kind, the *higher clergy*, was of a fundamentally
different nature. Its aim and object was

to serve not Christianity but *Politics*, not politics that are good and
true to society, wholesome and useful, but politics whose task and
aim it is to keep the people themselves in darkness, weakness,
misery, and destitution, in order to capture and use the strength of
the people, their means, their lives, and their whole existence to
the advantage of a small number of men who have divorced their
interests from those of the people. Such things cannot possibly be
done without keeping people under an unnatural yoke, and this
cannot be done without spreading over their souls a darkness that
paralyzes their power of thinking.

This requires lies of all kinds. It is very important to preach
the *doctrine of misery*: the conviction, said Almqvist, "must be
urged on them *that a miserable life on earth is the condition of
eternal bliss.* In this way they will receive full compensation
in the after-life for letting those *few* enjoy the good things of
this world."

Almqvist looked, however, further into the heavens, and
made the ironic comment, that he was sure that all these millions
of enslaved souls would also be exposed to aristocrats and prelates in another world; they would be told even there that misery
was again their lot and that true bliss ought to be put off till
yet another life." If aristocrats and prelates are allowed to
have their way, this bliss will undoubtedly *never* be realized
for the people themselves but will be *deferred* again and again
until a more suitable time." The upper classes, however, considered it quite proper for them to experience bliss even in this
life and to as high a degree as their organs were capable of
enjoying.

"*The clergy as a whole* has nothing to fear from the genius
of the age," said Almqvist, "but *Prelacy* has and must have."

We purposely say Prelacy, not *Prelates*. For as individuals and as
far as they can be imagined out of their prelatic context, they can

be both charming and respectable men. The only thing about them that we can wonder at is that they still want to remain prelates. (*AB*, April 1, 1842)

Almqvist again emphasized his old conviction that the higher clergy, the prelacy—as opposed to the lower clergy—were not in the service of Christianity but of politics, and he talked of "the aristocratic and prelatic authorities which are nothing but *scabies on the nations.*" This witty expression was taken up by Almqvist as a title for the article *"Om nationernas 'skabb'"* ("On the 'Scabies' of Nations," *AB*, April 5, 1842), in which he developed his views on hereditary nobility and the prelacy as well as the ingenious metaphor: just as aristocracy represented the improper, the false, and the morbid as opposed to what Almqvist called the rationally genuine nobility (the whole body of noble persons in a country: a class which really existed though not endowed with political rights), "so Prelacy stands in relation to the true and proper Clergy in a real Christian sense." Prelacy was also—to put it mildly—"a skin disease affecting the body of society, as well as the hereditary nobility, and to drive it out the Marsh Tea of common sense is needed and—for patients who prove to be quite inaccessible to reason—flowers-of-sulphur of jokes" (*AB*, April 5, 1842).

III   *On Hereditary and Representative Nobility*

The theological views in these last articles are chiefly concerned with church politics and bear witness to Almqvist's general political radicalism. His interest in electoral reform was very marked, and in the 1840s he persistently attacked the two upper estates of the Swedish parliament, the nobility and the clergy. When he referred to nobility he always opposed hereditary nobility to nobility of merit, and this is also the case in such a late newspaper article as *"Ärftligt och representativt adelskap ånyo formligt, men icke med särdeles framgång, försvarat av Tiden"* (Hereditary and Representative Nobility, Once More Defended Formally But Without Success by *Tiden*," *AB*, March 11, 1851). This is a polemic against a series of articles in the conservative newspaper, *Tiden* (*Time*). Almqvist predicted that "our Swedish nobility as an estate of its own with a personal right to representation founded on birth such as it is now should and will sooner or later disappear." It was to be wished that "the aristocracy based only on the accident of birth" might disappear and be replaced by true aristocracy which was that of personal distinction—"the advance of all Swedish citizens if possible, toward education, wealth, and influence."

And Almqvist continued to expound his theory with pedagogic clarity and lofty sentiment: "But could one not also call genius and mental excellence birth, and value them accordingly? In that case we should stand on truly natural ground, ennobled through man's own actions and raised to noble dignity."

He then demonstrated what fatal consequences the principle of an aristocracy of birth would produce if applied to natural science. Imagine it being maintained that the metal that had first been used was better than the metal that had later been freed from slag and impurities!

If somebody told us for instance that the iron or the copper that was used in the days of Abraham or Moses is baronial iron or noble copper, we should laugh in his face if we could prove to him that copper from Falun or iron from Österby was quite as good and quite as suitable for making horseshoes or horse-shoe nails or for plating ships, etc.

But surely the pine wood that the Ark was made of must have been of a nobler sort, Almqvist asked, and consequently coated with gold? Well, but then where is the Ark now?

It was the most honorable old tub that existed in the Old Testament; but nevertheless no vestiges of it remain in our day. In the same way the patented nobility is the golden tub of prejudices, and the time will come when the same thing will happen to it as to the Ark: no man will be able to say what has become of it. [. . .] The rational, noble, and laudable action is the one that ennobles men in the eyes of God and consequently also ought to do so in the eyes of the world. (*AB*, March 11, 1851)

IV *On the Literary Activity of Women and Old Friends*

The article, *"Fruntimmers författarskap"* ("Women's Literary Activities," *AB*, July 14, 1845) provides an excellent example of

Almqvist's elegant argumentation and confirms his liberal view of women's right to assert themselves in the same fields as men:

> We declare once and for all that we are no friend of those unsuccessful female writers of belles-lettres who are conventionally called *blue-stockings*: but we fear that many a male writer of belles-lettres may be called a *jack-boot* and rightly so: and we suggest provisionally that the latter name be adopted as a counterpart of the former, so that the two sexes may be equally entitled to inherit derogatory designations. Men ought to have an equal share of the bad as they do of the good. (*AB*, July 14, 1845)

Almqvist proceeds to discuss the difference between genius and mediocrity—without, however, discriminating between the sexes.

There is a connection between art and politics which had been present in Almqvist's writings from an early stage and became more and more frequent after "On the Poetry of Facts." Suffice it to mention *Sara Videbeck*, which combines artistic freedom with social purpose. In this connection there is another noteworthy article entitled, *"Några ord om herr Atterbom"* ("A Few Words on Mr. Atterbom," *AB*, July 3, 1847).

This article is a critical review of Atterbom's monograph on Per Elgström, a Phosphorist who had died at an early age. In his review Almqvist also speaks of the æsthetic significance of Phosphorism. He contrasts the Phosphorists' artistic renewal with their marked lack of political interest:

> They only wished to *sing* about freedom, love, and beauty; but did not want these in order to lead a better, deeper, and truer life than hitherto, within the sphere of human conditions on earth. On such things they looked down with scorn! [. . .]
> The inconsistency of the Phosphorists was that they refused society the political development toward the same liberty they had claimed for Poetry at least in the beginning; they became absolutists and extremists; consequently, their particular shade of poetry, Romanticism, got the bad reputation of belonging to a school of singers in the service of superstition and autocracy. (*AB*, July 3, 1847)

At the beginning of his review Almqvist gave a characterization of Atterbom, starting with the latter's polemic writings. Parts of it are worth reproducing:

Atterbom's lyre is and has always been charming. If his key has not sounded as true as for instance Tegnér's and consequently has not won so much sympathy, it is certainly due to his personal ill health, which we must regret but not criticize as a fault. If, in spite of being a poet, he had expressed his opinion on politics or polemized against tendencies in art and society that he had not approved of, that is not in itself a matter for blame, but his manner of proceeding deserves censure since he has allowed himself loose, sarcastic, often brutal attacks on doctrines, incidents, and persons [. . .]. We shall not embark on an investigation of the causes. His exasperated adversaries explain it quite simply by his being at one and the same time, in certain matters at least, very narrow-minded, conceited, and also extremely hypersensitive [. . .]. As for his notorious arrogance, [. . .] we are convinced of the genuine piety at the root of Mr. Atterbom's character, which does not allow to cherish pride before God or inveterate spite against human beings, though his bad temper, as we have seen, has made him quick to adopt on certain occasions a wasp's or a mosquito's readiness to sting. (*AB*, July 3, 1847)

Almqvist's characterization of his old friend's opinions and qualities, which he had known well for more than twenty-five years, is crushing and, in spite of its core of truth, unfair. Almqvist's own polemic technique is interesting to study. The basic principle is that, whatever the context, he opens with a vaguely positive appraisal of Atterbom, which he immediately takes back in the next sentence by expressing a negative, often downright opinion; the whole exercise is laced with insinuation.

Almqvist's subtle wording is often very telling in his disputes with old friends. For instance, he says of Geijer that he lives too much under the illusion "that he is making unprecedented new statements and that he is carrying them forward to decisive points. He shows this by the tone of affected stupidity behind which his presumptuousness is inadequately concealed, and of feigned insignificance which too clearly betrays his desire to be important" (*AB*, July 12, 1839). For further views on Almqvist's relationship with Geijer, see also p. 162.

Almqvist's review of the pamphlet "*Attarpska målet*" ("The Attarp Case") is most interesting. The facts of the reviewed lawsuit, which was published in book form in 1846, are that P. L. Ekwall, owner of the Attarp estate, died of arsenic poisoning and that the three women mentioned in the article were suspected of murder. Confessions and accusations were made and withdrawn. The outcome of the complicated lawsuit was that Mrs. Ekwall was acquitted for lack of conclusive evidence, her daughter Sofie Ekwall was sentenced to death, and the maid, Hedda Thorman, was sent to a house of correction. Later, in the Supreme Court, the sentences were reduced.

In his review Almqvist points out that this lawsuit outdoes most European *causes célèbres*. It is, however, his political and social commentary which is of particular interest:

Nobody can pretend to discern the real cause of the Attarp affair; but it is probably to be found in that demonic element which hovers over the whole of our civilization like a social Moloch, carrying off millions of victims every year, though it only occasionally leads up to arsenic poisoning, murders of whole families, and finally to the block, but much more often to mental poisonings, economic ravages, faded cheeks, broken hearts, and the destruction of many of life's flowers, which Providence created for its children but which this heathen god devours. (*AB*, December 22, 1846)

Thus the Attarp lawsuit was a criminal case that was not only intricate from a legal point of view but also extremely interesting psychologically. That Almqvist was fascinated by it is evident. In his article we find all the interests in crime and criminals, in death, in the mysterious and the sensational, that he showed throughout his writings. But he also dwelt on the guilt of society and matrimony, which he compared to the fatal Moloch. It is the author of *Sara Videbeck* who is viewing matrimony, and it is the author of *The Causes of European Discontent* who is leading us to understand that there is need for a general unmasking. When one reads this article it is difficult not to look ahead five years, to the fateful days in June 1851.

V *On the Practicability of Scandinavianism*

Almqvist's activity on behalf of Scandinavianism must also be mentioned. As we have already seen, he devoted many pages of journalism to the concept of the solidarity and unification of Scandinavia. His attitude was further strengthened during the six months he spent in Copenhagen in the fall of 1845 and the

winter of 1846. Almqvist was cordially received there; the letters
to his family speak of the pleasure he takes in being greeted
as an honored guest in the neighboring country. He renewed
old acquaintances and made new friends.

In Copenhagen in February 1846, Almqvist delivered his great
lecture, "On the Practicability of Scandinavianism" (published
in book form in 1846), an ingenious and far-seeing contribution
to the debate. What he has to say is governed by objectivity
and common sense. He sums up with a list of ten points.

The first three are closely connected; they refer to the geography, history, and language of Scandinavia. Almqvist the
teacher—who is seen in his most advantageous light in this
book—underlines the importance of giving, from the very earliest
years at school, a true and uniform presentation of the essential
unity of Scandinavia. As adults we can always use our powers
of reflection to understand the concept of Scandinavian unity.
"But this Unity stands more powerful, nay, ineffaceable, before
our minds, if it *has already come into existence as an instinctive
feeling*, an axiomatic basic thought in children's original way
of looking at things" ("On the Practicability of Scandinavianism," p. 5).

Of the ten points included in his practical suggestions, he
pays most attention to the first three. Almqvist looks on the
current teaching of geography as the charm of the map, which
should be extended concretely and colorfully beyond the boun-
daries of Sweden and color the fields of Denmark and Norway
as well.

Point two concerns history. Here also he demands of the
textbook a disposition that "treats the history of the Scandinavian
people, that is to say the history of the Nordic-speaking peoples,
as a whole" (p. 9). As a liberal Almqvist castigated the habit—
the bad habit—of older historians of confining themselves mainly
to lists of kings and biographies of rulers, and hoped that he
would live to see the history of the Scandinavian *people* instead
of the predominantly political history of dynasties.

The third point in Almqvist's lecture referred to the language.
Here, too, he pointed out the original unity but admitted that it
would certainly be impossible now to fuse Swedish and Danish
together in literature and writing. But it would be a good thing

if both languages were taught as distinct subjects throughout Scandinavia. As a lexicographer Almqvist also dreamed of the possibility of both languages being included in the same dictionary "simultaneously so that in a big dictionary that included dialects, a Swedish dictionary for instance, cognate Danish words with their various meanings would be entered as dialectal forms; and that in a Danish dictionary similar Swedish words would be included, but as dialectal variants" (p. 14). Here, too, it should be remembered, Almqvist had practical experience with his *Ordbok över svenska språket* (*Dictionary of the Swedish Language*) of 1840–42, planned on a large scale but never completed, and *A Swedish Grammar* (3rd ed. 1840). Of the three points mentioned here, Almqvist said that they were of such a character that they could be realized "at any time by any individual who wants to do so, without being hindered by any duty that might stand in his way" (p. 16). As for the remaining seven points which would also contribute to bringing Scandinavia together, he said that they could not be carried out by individuals but only by the governments of the two countries.

In point four he recommended a "*development of legal matters that is parallel and common to both countries.*" Almqvist pointed out that the original provincial laws of the Scandinavian peoples—brought to the fore in Sweden by Schlyter's great edition of the medieval laws which was just then in progress—"form a unique legal basis, free and different from the *Jus Romanum* contagion of the rest of Europe" (p. 17). The other practical points that Almqvist made, though with greater caution and sometimes with a certain hesitation, implied a customs union for the whole of Scandinavia, a common monetary unit, and a common post and passport administration. Under point eight—foreign affairs—he suggested an offensive and defensive alliance. A consequence of this was point nine proposing common training camps for the armed forces of the two countries. In that case "the thought would soon pervade Scandinavia that all of us have to stand or fall together" (p. 18).

Here Almqvist touched on a very sensitive topic which developments in the succeeding decades were to make still more sensitive.

The tenth and last point in Almqvist's program was more

comprehensive. It concerned "the unity of our *universities*." Almqvist first raised the question of creating a new Scandinavian university, a project that had also been proposed by Grundtvig to whom Almqvist refers. But the thought of a university with two headquarters and authorities—and all the competition for professorships and the academic quarrels that would thrive under such double rule—made Almqvist reject such a solution. One cannot help hearing a personal note in the reference to "possible collisions when appointing professors" (p. 19); quite likely, the controversies in connection with the Lund professorship of 1838 were all too fresh in Almqvist's memory. Instead he recommended a freer interchange of staff and students and mutual validity of Scandinavian academic examinations.

Summing up, Almqvist rightly pointed out: "Only a few years ago Scandinavianism was regarded *altogether* as an idle fancy. Now it has already gained so much ground that people even regard it as largely sensible and practical. This is enough for a start" (p. 21).

His peroration exalted both the practice and the poetry of Scandinavianism:

> I thank you for according me the privilege that is seldom bestowed on a Swede, to be allowed to speak his own language and yet be understood without translation, although he is not speaking within the boundaries of Sweden. Oh, I was forgetting myself—I know one thing—I remember: I am in Sweden now that I am in Copenhagen. May a Dane soon come to see us in Stockholm and speak there, in his own native language, about the common subject so dear to us. He will utter Danish words, but the people of Stockholm will listen to them as to Swedish sentences. For the thoughts and the words now are neither those of Denmark nor of Sweden: they are those of Scandinavia. Its soul has awakened. (p. 21)

In his journalism and political writings, Almqvist persistently brought up the great problems of his day. In his attitudes and opinions, he was often inconvenient to those in power. At his best moments he was a brilliant and witty polemist; he certainly owes his admirable journalism to the fact that he was prompt, lucid, and convincing.

He was also a social visionary, evidenced by his interests in the emancipation of women, the representation reform, Scandinavianism, and many other social and political questions. He was one of few who were able to distinguish the finest veins and nerves in the heart of prejudices, and he helped to erase some of them. Like his literary production, his journalism is still of great interest.

Indeed, Almqvist is our contemporary.

CHAPTER 11

European Discontent and Sober Criticism

I Sviavígamál *and* Mythopoiesis

THE last few years of the 1840s were not very productive for Almqvist so far as his fiction was concerned—at least not in comparison with the flood of work of the '30s and the early '40s. His newspaper articles and musical compositions provide the most interesting evidence of his activity.

In 1849 and '50 he published the last two volumes of the imperial octavo edition. As already stated, the second volume contained mainly earlier works of high quality such as "*Songes,*" *Sviavígamál,* and a few symbolic sagas from the 1820s. The controversial and partially new subject matter came in the third volume, the first part of which is *The Causes of European Discontent.*

The most important component of the second volume is of course *Songes,* which now after twenty years at last reached the public in an edition printed and approved by the author. *Songes* has, however, already been treated in detail, so let us pass on to *Sviavígamál.*

Sviavígamál is a cycle of Nordic sagas, comprising "Håtuna Saga," "Sigtuna Saga," "Valtuna Saga," and "Odensala Saga." A kind of introduction is furnished by a short study, "Commemoration on the First of April," in which the epic setting of *Sviavígamál* is indicated. There is no conclusion. The last saga, "Odensala Saga," is suddenly brought to an end by a provocative, "And . . . ," in harmony with the aesthetic theory propounded in "Dialogue on How To Finish Pieces." Richard Furumo, the narrator, translates the title *Sviavígamál* as "Sweden's war poem or heroic history."

158

The beginning of *Sviavígamál* recounts the arrival of Odin and the Æsir in the beautiful Lake Mälar region. The Nordic gods are said to come from Asia, whence the name of "Æsir," and thus far Almqvist follows the theories accepted by his contemporaries. But at the same time he flavors the whole account with what might be called double romantic irony: Almqvist makes the god Odin take Snorre Sturlasson's *Heimskringla* as a model for his exploits, for in his omnipotence Odin can read in advance all the books that are going to be written and he amuses himself by arranging his life in accordance with Snorre Sturlasson's story.

The far fetched etymologies that he reels off so freely are also part of the narrator's playfulness; thus he derives "waltz" from the "*Val*" dance" and "tobacco" from "tabu."

But in *Sviavígamál* there are also examples of Almqvist's finest prose, and in general this remarkable work deserves a much larger reading public. Henry Olsson has said that something of the virgin freshness of the morning of the creation pervades these primeval scenes, and he has finely characterized the atmosphere of both golden age and primitive cruelty in *Sviavígamál*: "In the strawbinding rites of the Jumala girls there is a subtle sense of magic; highly suggestive, too, are the bloody, paganly brutal scenes of human sacrifices in "Valtuna Saga," for instance Fyse's death among the voracious pike."[1]

The second volume of the imperial octavo edition also contains *Mythopoiesis*, three tales told by Herr Hugo. Here he makes a detailed exposition of the difference between Richard Furumo's poetry and poetic view, and his own. Richard's poetry is "reality and truth" whereas Herr Hugo's is mythical poetry or poetry of myths, which is close to dreams. It represents an earlier stage of poetry at which art was unwilling or unable to "take reality as such poetically." This mythical poetry is symbolic: "it does not describe life but depicts something that is meant to stand for life." It is a kind of poetry that, according to Herr Hugo, predominates in oriental, medieval European, and modern German (and Swedish phosphoristic) art. In other words, Almqvist describes here his own earlier poetry, and of the three tales that Herr Hugo mentions, the first two had as a matter of fact already been printed by Almqvist at the beginning of the 1820s: "Goldbird in Paradise" and "Rosaura." The third tale had not been printed before but seems to have been written at about the same time and is called "Arctura."

The second volume is completed by *Sober Criticism*, a short comedy in the style of Molière, in which Almqvist surveys his literary production. This important work will be discussed later (p. 169f.).

II   The Causes of European Discontent

The third volume of the imperial octavo edition was published in December 1850. It opens with *The Causes of European Discontent*, an essay at which he had been working ever since the 1820s, trying out one version after another. Its basic ideas probably go back even further and were touched on in the little pamphlet, *What is Love?* of 1816 (cf. above, p. 14). In more advanced form he had pursued these lines of thought in *Sara Videbeck* and in his newspaper articles after 1839. As Werin points out, Almqvist here claims to be presenting *politics of facts*, a counterpart to his literary program. The essay consists of three sections or books: an introduction with six chapters, then the so-called "green manuscript" divided into two parts containing six and eight letters, respectively.

The first five letters were printed in 1838, but the whole edition was destroyed. In the spring of 1847 Almqvist published the first six letters in *Jönköpingsbladet* in a series of articles under the headline, *"Om orsakerna till det närvarande släktets verkliga eller inbillade olyckor"* ("On the Causes of the Real or Imagined Misfortunes of the Present Generation"). In the same year he resumed the printing of the essay in book form and got as far as the eleventh letter before he stopped and destroyed this edition also.

Finally the essay was published in the third volume of the imperial octavo edition of 1850.

The essay is unfinished insofar as it was intended to deal in three large sections with the family, the church, and the state, but in fact it treats only the first subject. It is true that the author promised to write about the church and the state in two succeeding sections, but he never managed to fulfill this promise. His way of dealing with that part of society represented by the family was, however, effective.

The introductory frame is presented at the Hunting Seat where at lilac time Herr Hugo institutes a Council of State "in the realm of the spirit, in the kingdom of intelligence." One of the members presents a collection of letters called "the green manuscript" because the letters were written on green note paper. With echoes from "Dialogue on How To Finish Pieces," we are told that

the end is cut off, and I do not know if any more letters have been written on the same subject by that hand. Thus the collection of letters is a fragment as far as the end is concerned, but otherwise it is complete and contains all that is needed for the basic ideas. On the other hand further development of these ideas can and should continue forever. (*CW*, XVI, p. 21)

In the first letter the narrator speaks of the discontent and its cause: "It is something inexpressible that is lacking in the whole of our culture" (*CW*, XVI, p. 23). Conditions are miserable and unsatisfactory. What can be done? Medicine is not used in the right way, reprimands are without avail. Writers cannot advise us. We have not yet been told what the real problems are, but everybody knows that something is going to happen: "The future of Europe is waiting on all our doorsteps, wanting to come in. Anyone who does not unlock his door to the knocking visitor will get his door smashed in—and he will be lucky if the splinters do not fly into his face" (*CW*, XVI, p. 26).

The next letter deals with the human being, the individual versus society and its laws. The times are blamed for advancing toward lawlessness and immorality, but that is a mistake. If we want to do away with unnecessary and harmful laws, that does not imply that our goal is lawlessness, and the narrator stresses that it is far more important to search out, pursue, and correct the crimes of the state than those of the *individual*. "No baseness can sink to greater depths than those pertaining to the law itself" (*CW*, XVI, p. 28).

The *fundamental problem* is this: "People are forced into a violent conflict between what the established outward principles of society demand of them, on the one hand, and their true

inner humanity on the other. Which of them are they to obey?
That is the curse of life on earth" (*CW*, XVI, p. 29).

As matters stand now people will come off badly in both
cases. If—against their inner conviction and nature—they obey
absurd rules, they will be depressed and unhappy. If they do
not obey them, they are called criminals. *"Is it right that society
should be allowed* to confront people with such alternatives?
No! And it is against this that the giants of today have risen,
and they are not to be silenced" (*CW*, XVI, p. 30).

The narrator's hope is that education will "gradually supersede
the ordinary criminal laws" (*CW*, XVI, p. 31)—a line of thought
which relates strikingly to the essay, "On the Treatment of
Criminals."

In this letter, Almqvist seizes the opportunity—but without
mentioning names—of gibing at Geijer whose conversion to
liberal political views he considered tactically justified, but
too late:

We have also seen how one of the self-appointed martyrs has
become converted after long vociferation, only to find to his grief
that time has passed him by. He is annoyed, he goes *running along
behind,* hoping at least to be given a chance of riding in the back
seat of time's chariot, if nothing else. We see him there, not unlike
a drunken footman, boasting of his own exploits, and even railing
at those who have always followed the course he is now trying
to enter upon. (*CW*, XVI, p. 34)

For Almqvist's relationship with Geijer, see also p. 152.
According to Almqvist, Geijer, like many of his contemporaries,
did not understand the spirit of the times. A magnificent metaphor served to illustrate this: It is when the oarsman unexpect-
edly finds himself enveloped in sea mist and can no longer see
the shore.

How shall he row? He is fortunate if he can still see a friendly
star twinkling through the fog for his guidance. A few experienced
sailors have what is called the compass in their hearts; they can
find their way to the shore even in the darkness of the night. But
such men are rare. (*CW*, XVI, p. 36)

Letter number three bears the title, "The Basis of Revolution." Here the clever narrator began by associating the fight of the early Christians for the poor and lowly with the political movement of his own day: he pointed out that in both cases the important thing was our common equality before God, the law, and grace (*CW*, XVI, p. 40).

The narrator was not an advocate of subversion, but of improvement. It was not true that "people want uprising and subversion. People claim the liberty to live as God has meant them to live" (*CW*, XVI, p. 41).

In the fourth letter Almqvist divides the society of his day into ordinary people and the mob. The people were, defined by Almqvist's bold arithmetic, what remains "when one deducts the *mob* from the whole of the population" (*CW*, XVI, p. 44). The mob might be both disguised (certain superior, learned, educated, and enlightened men); and undisguised (that is, common hooligans; this mob was dreadful but better than the disguised mob). The mob was agreed in wanting a dead, petrified society. The people, on the other hand, were in favor of progress, they wanted a living society. The renewal was at hand, "the stripping is beginning, the masks are being pulled off" (*CW*, XVI, p. 49; cf. "On the Poetry of Facts": "the last hour of the masquerade is striking").

The important letter number six is entitled "The Main Point." The narrator says that one should not only grumble but also propose remedies. But first we must "concentrate all the thousand rays of complaints on to one great focal point, on to a main question, the chief concern" (*CW*, XVI, p. 54).

This main point is:

"The human being has a clear, inalienable right, the right to live in the sense intended by creation. *This means that everybody is to be allowed to follow the course proper to his or her true character*" (*CW*, XVI, p. 55).

The causes of the great European discontent were that people were not allowed to exercise this inalienable right. What the European revolution was rising against was the idea of authority and convention.

The right of humans to follow their own *course* is illustrated by an ingenious comparison with Kepler's calculation of the

course of the planet Mars. Kepler's work had valuable consequences for astronomy, but "nevertheless I hope for so much
common sense as to recognize that for human beings, it is still
more important to find *the true course of their own lives.* Finding
this may be as tremendously difficult as people say. Nevertheless,
it is a person's only main concern" (*CW*, XVI, p. 60).

The plan for his investigation of the matter was given in
the second part of the green manuscript:

The bulk of all human conditions can be divided into three
large groups:

1. Life in the *family*—the relationship between man and woman.
This forms a human unit on a minute scale, but constituting the
true basis and the real home for all the rest.

2. Life in the *congregation*—the relationship between God and
the individual, which forms a unit on the largest scale, constituting
the ideal basis and enabling all the rest to exist.

3. Life in the *state*—the relationship between people and government, which forms a unit of medium size; constituting the necessary
means for all the rest.

By the word *society* I understand all the three units together
forming a whole. (*CW*, XVI, p. 63)

Of these three relationships Almqvist now examines the first,
that between man and woman, and this takes up the next
eight letters—that is to say, the rest of *The Causes of European
Discontent.*

It is chiefly the question of marriage and the wedding ceremony that was analyzed, with frequent reference to *Sara
Videbeck.* Almqvist insisted that there must be sincere love and
spiritual agreement between woman and man contracting to
live together. The imperfection of the institution of marriage
at that time was quite clear: it sanctioned a union the spiritual
sense of which was not known; it made an absurd distinction
between right and wrong in sexual matters; it facilitated deceit
between the parties; it compelled them to make promises that
could not (or should not) be kept; it entailed an improper use
of ceremonies, prayers, and kind words. Regarding the improper use of ceremonies and prayers, Almqvist gave a cruel
and striking example:

Everybody must admit that the most beautiful, the most heavenly prayers cannot succeed in making white black, or black white. In stating this one does not in the least disparage a solemn act; one fully acknowledges in all sincerity its essential holiness and beauty; one only says that it does not do what it does not do. If, for example, a thief breaks into a house to steal but then proceeds to fold his hands over the stolen goods and say a prayer, then this prayer certainly does not cease to be good and beautiful in itself, but one must point out that it cannot possibly transform the stolen goods into legitimate property. Also, if a robber—as often happens in parts of Italy—says seven Ave Maria, or recites his rosary nine times over before rushing out to attack the victim he has picked out to rob, then we do not regard this hold-up as good, lawful, or religious despite the preceding ceremonial performance of a kind of religious ritual. (*CW*, XVI, p. 83)

Almqvist also pointed out that the wedding ceremony had a social purpose—different from any other church ceremony: the object of the wedding was "to compel people to continue living together for life, whatever the true nature of the mutual feelings and spiritual love of the parties may be" (*CW*, XVI, p. 85).

In order to remedy matters, Almqvist demanded that the law be changed: away with all weddings or similar contracts. With the help of the law a new system—the *Sara Videbeck* system—must be introduced instead, based on education, economic independence, and personal freedom.

Young people must be taught what is right and wrong in relations between man and woman.

Women and children must be made economically independent: like the man, the woman must have full right of ownership and use of everything that she possesses and must never forfeit this right through any relationship with another person. Among other things, Almqvist also proposed that, on a man's death, a third of all his property should go to a national fund, a sort of children's insurance fund, intended to guarantee that all children received a reasonable allowance. Almqvist was anxious to point out that this project was not intended to restrict the right of ownership, only to alter the system of inheritance. "It is not the slightest encroachment on any individual's right to manage and use his property in his lifetime (thus it is not part of the so-called phalanstère idea or the sort of communism which would bring about the most abject slavery, through the abolition of individualism in economic matters)" (*CW*, XVI, p. 130).

Finally, Almqvist demanded that personal liberty be safeguarded. He wrote an introductory note about the existing regulations for servants, which he attacked violently. He argues very cleverly that *everybody* must have political rights:

> To exclude the so-called serving class is quite absurd and at the same time extremely dangerous in the long run. Remember: all the reasons which once spoke in favor of the middle class entering the field of political rights at the side of hierarchy and aristocracy, exactly the same or similar and quite as good reasons now speak in favor of the serving class being included. That this involves an upheaval is quite true. There was also a great stir when "the third estate" reached a position of influence within the State. It was subversive! But for what? Of what? Of a bad state of affairs which through this "upheaval" had to give way to a better. The same is true now. *The serving class must have and will get political rights* (a share in representation, the right to send delegates to take part in legislation, in fixing tax contributions, etc.), and that applies to women as well. (*CW*, XVI, p. 132)

Almqvist maintains that things must change so that nobody has the right to retain any person who is of age, against the latter's will, whether in marriage or employment. But it must be a child's right and duty, until it comes of age, to stay with its mother.

Of course, the ideas that Almqvist presents in *The Causes of European Discontent* were in some measure those of his time and—as research has shown—they have their counterparts in the works of other European writers and philosophers. The French Count Saint-Simon and his doctrine, saint-simonism, spring to mind. Saint-Simon was a radical and wanted to proclaim a general brotherhood, which he called the universal association. He was deeply discontented with European civilization and believed, among other things, that the right of inheritance should be public, not private.

Another name to be mentioned is that of Robert Owen, a

Welsh merchant who founded a communist colony in New Harmony, Indiana, in 1824. On the other hand, there is no evidence to indicate that Almqvist knew anything about Marx; nevertheless, revolutionary activity was given adequate coverage by *Aftonbladet*, and in *Jönköpingsbladet* Almqvist himself had published a series of articles, *"Den stora läxan"* ("The Great Lesson"), in March 1848.

One name with which Almqvist was clearly acquainted was that of the French clerk, Charles Fourier, the first nineteenth-century socialist to condone extramarital sex relations. Arguments for "free love" were also advanced by the group of German authors from the 1830s and 1840s known as *"Das junge Deutschland,"* especially Karl Gutzkow, but Almqvist was very anxious not to be too closely associated with them. Finally, on the marriage question, there are definite indications that both Rousseau and Swedenborg exerted a strong influence upon Almqvist in his youth. And throughout his adult life, evidently, he was quite familiar with the issues of the day.

From what has been said it is also clear that the central focus of Almqvist's reflections in *The Causes of European Discontent* was woman. He repeatedly raises the question of woman's position in marriage and society with a fervor and perspicacity that are quite remarkable. It has been pointed out by Westman Berg that, in *The Causes of European Discontent*, Almqvist argues a line of feminism that favors matriarchy.[2] It is the woman—and the child—that he places at the fore; the man is the least important member of the trio.

But it is not only Almqvist the feminist we encounter here; it is above all Almqvist the seriously committed liberal unmasking all varieties of social and political inequities. The story of the origin of *The Causes of European Discontent* is—as already indicated—a very long one. In a letter to J. A. Hazelius of September 1827, Almqvist wrote that he was revolving such radical thoughts in his mind that they alarmed him. And in another letter to the same party, probably written in April 1839, he enclosed the first two sheets of "a work that contains what, for more than thirty years, I have been thinking out—that's nothing!—nay, have lived through, and seen in thousands of people that I have known" (*Letters*, p. 142).

The Causes of European Discontent is based on personal experiences, but also on personal convictions that had found expression in his fiction and newspaper articles long before this essay was at last published as the alarums of the February Revolution had already sounded the last hour of masquerade.

III   *Comedies in Prose*

After *The Causes of European Discontent*, in the third volume of the imperial octavo edition, come "Why Do You Travel?," *Sara Videbeck*, and a new revision of *Murnis*, works already dealt with (see pp. 125 f., 121–30, and 34–37).

The volume concludes with *The Silk Hare of Hagalund* and *The Purple Count*, two comedies in prose—or "dramatic stories" as Almqvist calls them in a letter from America. Earlier he had described them as amusing trifles "about a 'splendid idea' for avoiding all kinds of unnecessary domestic chores in the home, and greatly improving a certain aspect of the economy."[3] The splendid idea is to build a gigantic hotel to replace individual family households; according to one of the principal characters, this not only yields financial profit but also has important social effects. Above all, women will have time to develop spiritually:

> In addition to other good effects, this would also have the great advantage that families would escape in their homes all the vexations, difficulties, and inconveniences that arise in connection with the kitchen and the acquisition and preparation of food. Women who are now so largely occupied with this and who, as many people believe, were created almost exclusively to do the cooking, would escape from this chore unless the person's natural aptitude led her solely and directly to it. People would get rid of the crude and absurd prejudice that womanliness, grace, and morality are restricted to certain occupations and would vanish if these were done away with; as though their charm would not on the contrary flourish still more, or at least remain what it is if women were allowed to devote themselves more frequently to mental activity according to the genius each individual has and the way she develops it. (*CW*, XVI, p. 386)

Obviously, Almqvist refers to experiments and utopias of his own day, but at the same time he allows economic and social successes to result from the efforts of one of the characters: the capitalist, director-general Westermarck.

In *The Purple Count*, in which the gigantic hotel has become a reality, a multilateral and collective love affair develops between two young couples: Cavalry Captain Adrian Westermarck, with his beautiful cousin Augusta Swifton, and "the purple count," Leonard Almsköld with the enlightened baroness, Emilie Liljenstjerna. Emilie, who loves both gentlemen, is at the beginning engaged to Adrian, who grants Leonard permission to take her over without himself sacrificing either her or Augusta. Emilie collects declarations of love from both Adrian and Leonard and sums up in content, "We all love each other here."

IV   Sober Criticism

Sober Criticism is a short play in which Almqvist discusses his own writings, his fictional characters, the message (or lack of message) in his works, and certain artistic principles. In the play he explicitly acknowledges Molière's *Critique de l'école des femmes* as his model. Furthermore, he translates long, relevant passages of Molière's play word for word, changing only the names and titles. It is doubtful whether Almqvist's adaptation should be called a translation or an imitation; but it would seem more accurate to regard it as an imitation. Almqvist frequently refers to his model in footnotes and also indicates which elements are taken from Molière's one-act play and which are his own.

The plot of *Sober Criticism* is quickly summarized. In its nine scenes, three ladies and four gentlemen carry on a conversation about the *Wild Rose* books.

In her salon the sensible Uranie, who is interested in human nature, receives her friend Elise, a young lady who is more severe in her criticism. They are joined by the lady Climène, out of favor with Uranie, and maliciously described by Elise's venomous tongue as stupid and affected, "using this expression in its worst sense" (*CW*, XV, p. 277). Climène has just come from a recitation of some *Wild Rose* rhapsodies where she was badly shocked by what she heard. This initiates the debate in

Uranie's salon on the *Wild Rose* poet and his works, which lasts to the end of the play.

The male contingent that joins in includes Abbé Sganarelle and Librarian-General Gorgibus, both depicted as ignorant and ridiculous; also the self-satisfied poet Lysidas, characterized by conceit and professional jealousy; and finally Dorante, a young man endowed with good sense and objectivity and hence to be regarded as Almqvist's mouthpiece. In this function he is supported by the outspoken Uranie and the sarcastic Elise.

The grouping is obvious: three votes for the Wild Rose author; four against him. Generally speaking, the characters are presented as black and white.

This strange artifice is something Molière owes to Cervantes; we may say that the embryo of this technique is found in *Don Quixote* (I:6), in the incident in which the parish priest suspends the burning of the books and says a few appreciative words about Cervantes and the latter's pastoral novel, *Galatea*.

Molière, on the other hand, has found few imitators. However, his technique may be said to be related to a form of narrative technique practiced by various exponents of Romantic irony. In Swedish literature, Almqvist is the only known imitator of Molière in this respect.

There is plenty of printed and unprinted material to show how skillfully Almqvist analyzes and annotates his own works. Reference has already been made to "Dialogue on How To Finish Pieces," "The Return," *Monography*, and also to Almqvist's newspaper articles and certain of his letters. But as an effort at examining his entire literary production, *Sober Criticism* is unique among Almqvist's works. Add to this the fact that the examination is clothed in fictional form and made the subject of a play, and *Sober Criticism* becomes unique in Swedish literature.

CHAPTER 12

Epilogue in Exile

I *Letters from the United States*

DURING his years in exile, 1851–66, Almqvist did a good
deal of writing. In the extant letters to his family, his impressions of the new milieu and new continent often take the
form of brilliant travel documentaries, amusing and informative.
They also provide the most important documentation we have
for the last fifteen years of his life. His poems from these years,
some of which leave a distinctly autobiographical impression,
may also have something to add.

The first surviving letter was datelined St. Louis, Missouri,
October 4, 1852. He had arrived there in March, the same
year. The letter was addressed to his daughter and—like the
following letters—it bears witness to Almqvist's intense interest
in his family in Sweden, his hunger for news and contact: "Please
just go on describing in your letters every detail in the same
simple way. General observations may be respectable and all
very fine, but it is in the very details I see your life, and that is
exactly what I want" (*Letters*, p. 220).

We find roughly the same guiding principle in his own letters.
His first letters from America in particular are little travelogues—
often of the same standard as his best from the '20s and '30s.
They are full of enthusiastic descriptions and cheerfully recorded
details from a new and unknown continent, amusing and
instructive.

I shall give here a few examples of Almqvist's vivid and
penetrating descriptions of the environments in which he lived;
these contribute considerably to our knowledge of life in the
United States in the 1850s:

It is really no small mystery how a stranger who comes to an
entirely unfamiliar city can immediately feel at home there and

171

have the necessary information and skill to enable him to survive, make a fairly good impression, not have to pay through the nose and be swindled, and not perish from boredom or distress as in a desert. The secret is always to be entirely natural and at the same time polite wherever you go. You must also be fairly well dressed, and above all, not be shy either in your physiognomy or your heart. [. . .] The American way is to be polite in a manner that is often very impolite, and in this lies a certain piquancy which is attractive to many. When a German, on the other hand, is unrestrained, he is nearly always free in a rude way: this may be due to his honesty which forces him as a matter of conscience to be rude in every instance if rudeness is his general manner, and this leads directly to coarseness. As for smart clothes, being too elegant will not do here; you are regarded as a dandy, a good-for-nothing who does not do anything [. . .]. But being dirty is much worse. [. . .] A genuine American must change his underwear every day, or every two days, at the very least every three days. The poorest workman and the richest banker have shirts of very different quality, but both must wear them newly washed, that is why laundry is among the workman's heaviest items of expenditures. [. . .] The Americans will not put up with bearded chins, whiskers, or moustaches. Everything must be freshly shaved, otherwise it is not *comme il faut*. The whole physiognomy must be as smooth as a mirror. If a man with the beginning of a beard comes into the company of Americans, they consider him crazy, under the influence of a caprice, or just escaped from the calabouse. With the Germans, by contrast, a beard is a recommendation: the more bushy the whiskers, the bigger the *Schnurrbart* (moustache), the more dreadful the pointed beard, the better: if one's face is hairy up to one's eyes, that is the summit of perfection. Yet all this growth must not be tidily combed, tended, or neatly arranged, but tangled or matted. Otherwise the man is not considered quite reliable, but is suspected of being a secret supporter of the European courts. The worse the color of the beard—for instance, if it is a mixture of gray hair and reddish yellow and blackish yellow—the better the man. The gray hairs show that he has *"ein deutsches Herz"* (which is something unique, and which, in the opinion of the Germans, does not exist anywhere but in themselves); the blackish yellow bristles show that he is a true Democrat of the Kinkel type, and the reddish yellow hairs that he is as outstandingly brave as Hecker himself. The Irish also often sport beards, not long ones but trimmed with scissors because very often they cannot afford a shave, and anyway, they hate soap and everything connected with soap. [. . .] A Yankee prefers not to wear a necktie in summer, his usually very long, thin, scraggy and bony neck is bare, which perfectly matches his generally very lean and pale face, hollow cheeks, and thin lips. As he is more often than not fairly long-legged, he frequently bears a certain resemblance to a crane out on business. (*Letters,* pp. 223–26)

But Almqvist discusses not only Yankees and the national traits of various Europeans; he also encounters individuals who are far more exotic than the Germans, however bearded these may be, namely Indians.

Some time ago a whole procession of them headed by their chief, *Chicito,* passed through here on their way to Austin (the capital of Texas), where they wanted to negotiate with the Governor and obtain some land and trade concessions, which he granted them. The company consisted of sixteen persons, all of them mounted, and among them several squaws. They would have been very handsome if they had not had the disgusting habit of painting the whole of their faces red, blue, yellow, etc. They were in their way richly dressed; there was certainly no question of shirts or chemises, but their bodies were covered with the most gaudy and strange pieces of cloth (quilts, bits of coats, bandages, plaits of horsehair eight feet long) and lots of glass ornaments, polished brass, tin trinkets and the like. They never wear anything on their heads; even in the most glaring sun they ride without hats or caps, but they have thick, shining, absolutely straight hair flowing in the wind and falling down around their shoulders. From their dress one cannot tell any difference between a man and a woman. They had an American agent, a certain Mr. Lüntzel with them, as interpreter and helper. Formerly the forefathers of these savages, or so-called *Indians,* possessed the whole of Texas, and their hunting expeditions took them down to the coast (the Gulf of Mexico): the very place where the Europeans generally land now was one of their chief centers. That is why it is still called *Indianola* after them. Higher up, in the northwest of Texas, there still live warlike and dangerous Indians, especially those belonging to to the *Comanche* tribe. Every year they shoot and scalp Europeans who have come in search of the rich gold and silver mines west of the rivers *Pedernales* and *Llano,* near *San Saba* and *Sierra Guadalupa.* (*Letters,* p. 244 f.)

In the same letter—of November 1853—Almqvist told of an adventurous journey up the Mississippi River, a remarkable feat in itself as he was now sixty years old:

The steamships here are built in a quite extraordinary way. Here the lower deck which is in Sweden the most important area, is used only for cargo and goods. Above it there are two floors, and the whole boat looks like a floating house. Thus the first floor (corresponding to the "*däck*" in Sweden) is built over and covered by the second floor. The most distinguished passengers travel on this, the upper story; they have to pay a lot of money for the passage and are given sumptuous meals. Ordinary people travel on the lower—steerage—floor, they do not have to pay much and have to live at their own expense, that is to say, they hardly eat anything during the whole journey. Like most of the passengers, I was in this group. If one takes in supplies, one can have a good time, of course. On such journeys I usually buy some bread and cheese, that is all. Getting sleeping accommodation depends on whether there are any women on board, they always have priority. Anyway, the sleeping accommodation only consists of cubicles divided off by wooden partitions, in which one lies down on boards. If one has brought a mattress one can be comfortable. I never brought one. Otherwise one spends the night sitting on a trunk or chair talking to all the passengers gathered around the stove or sleeping when possible. On these journeys I have slept very well as a rule, wrapped in my cloak, leaning against anything I could find. When I have got too hungry, I have filled my pipe, which has been my permanent consolation on my travels; the tobacco appeases my stomach for a while. Toward morning the womenfolk wake up and put the coffee-kettle on the stove. Then it is easy to get a cup of coffee (without milk and often without sugar). (*Letters*, p. 237 f.)

This unsentimental image of the tired but interested traveler wrapped in his cloak, stilling his hunger with tobacco and patiently waiting for the dawn in order to beg a cup of coffee, seems like an illustration from "The Significance of Swedish Poverty."

Finally, we find in the same letter an impression of the scenery which, with the help of his astronomic speculations, reminds him of his lost Sweden:

There is very little that can compare in beauty with a Texan evening in the fall: here the sky is a darker blue, the stars glitter gloriously, and the moon—when it is full—shines with a stronger and brighter light than in Sweden. But for me it is melancholy to see my beloved constellation Charles's Wain lie half-way down toward the forest whereas, in Sweden, it stands almost straight above your head. That reminds me how far we are separated from one another. There are also several glittering constellations here that you cannot see in Sweden. I find them beautiful and precious enough—but I always think: Alas, you don't belong to me. (*Letters*, p. 247)

II On Swedish Rhymes

Several preserved manuscripts also provide tangible evidence of his literary activity during his years of exile. The most important of these is a manuscript of 1,438 folio pages, copied out beautifully in different colored inks, entitled *On Swedish Rhymes*.[1] It is essentially a dissertation on Swedish rhymes and prosody, the line of reasoning being interspersed with examples in the form of new poems by Almqvist himself. The setting is the same as that of *The Book of the Wild Rose*: the Löwenstjerna Hunting Seat. There Herr Hugo and his ever increasing staff of counsellors and reporters carry on an endless conversation on the mysteries of versification with digressions on language, stylistics, national character, literature, and indeed, everything under the sun.

A large part of *On Swedish Rhymes* is taken up by the section "Sesemana," a collection of 576 poems the title of which alludes to Hans Jakob Seseman, a well-known second-rate Stockholm poet. The Seseman poems are of great personal interest, not least for the way in which they supplement the information given in the letters. Many feelings and moods experienced in America which have not found expression in the letters are here presented in bizarre, at times absurd form. Erik Gamby has discussed this sort of double entry bookkeeping and has come to the conclusion that in these poems, Almqvist "confessed his most secret thoughts" and that consequently they provide a "more naked and truthful picture of Almqvist than do any other sources."[2] Even if this is stated rather categorically—we have no sources from these years except the poems and the letters—it is a fact that certain poems undoubtedly seem to give an impression of deep personal experience. This is especially true of the concluding poem, with its simple, naïve, pathetic beauty. I shall return to it.

Simple things and the necessaries of life are the favorite topics in these poems from the years in America. It is often a strong craving for certain dishes or certain sensations of taste that finds its way into poetry. The dream of Swedish gooseberries is associated with a late echo of happy Scandinavianism in the frequently cited poem:

> Is there a man on this earthly round
> Who has had the favor
> Of enjoying the flavor
> Of gooseberries, big, delicious, and sound
> Without exclaiming: I never tasted the like before.
> A shipload of oranges or a batch
> Of yellow Seville fruit would not match
> The gooseberries which tempt and please much more.
> What is offered by Africa?
> What presented by America?
> What by Asia or the West?
> I openly defy the rest.
> Scandinavia is marvelous, though.
> Only in Sweden do Swedish gooseberries grow.
> > (*Poems in Exile,* p. 53)

Other poems deal with the boon of clean clothes and shoes without holes.

A subject that often recurs is loneliness and friendlessness, doubly hard for a man like Almqvist, accustomed to being a leader and central figure, surrounded by friends:

"Now I have no friends left! not one was moved to tears at my ruin."

The Almqvist who had previously written about the sun and the moon and who had described the creation in the beautiful myth, "The Tears of Beauty," now laments his desolation in the darkness of exile:

> A moon that in the middle of the night is shining
> Is better than a sun just out of sight.
> I am walking on a lonely path, the wind is whining.
> I have no sun, no moon, no light.
> Oh, Lord, I beseech thee.
> Have mercy upon me,
> Poor man, and help me soon,
> Lend me a little moon![3]

Death through drowning had been a motif in Almqvist's earlier literary works; particularly noteworthy is the *songe*, "The Drowned Swimmer." During his years of exile a bitter poem is added:

> Where is the lake where one can be drowned
> In peace and quiet, even with pleasure,
> And without the unpleasant stench?
> Where no corpses cover the bottom of the lake
> With nastiness? nor any dead fish
> Or musty rascally crayfish that died without sense or discipline?
> If there is such a lake, I will go there quite soon
> Without noise, din, and the crowd
> And in its pure water I will find sweet heaven.
>
> (*Poems in Exile,* p. 99)

Corpses and impurity stop his alter ego but his longing for the deep and his assurance of heaven are still there.

Almqvist achieves a striking finale with the pathetic naïvely beautiful Seseman epilogue:

> Now, Father in heaven, I would have a word with you.
> I am speaking open-heartedly and freely
> As we belong to the same family, and you
> Are one who has mercy on us.
> Therefore I will tell you what I am going to do:
> I will sing and paint to myself and alone,
> Quite silently and quietly,
> And never do the humblest creature in the world the least harm.
> I love you, oh my heavenly great Father!
> If you will believe me in my simple lines,
> And I also love your dear Son, and all your other sons,
> Whatever people may call them throughout the world.
> I also love your Spirit in words and acts:
> When elm-trees and lime-trees whisper, then I hear your Spirit, too,
> Like the roaring of high waterfalls.
> You and your Spirit have strewn my path with blossoms
> And also with thistles which go with the roses.
> Red roses and white, and blue, oh, God of life, and green leaves!
> Have you not adorned my meadows for me?
> And made my groves so beautiful?

As for me I am only hay, mown and cut for fodder:
And therefore now—whenever you please,
Oh, my good Father, I will die!   (*Poems in Exile*, p. 100 f.)

There is an atmosphere of resignation and peace about these
lines which brings an echo from "The Poet's Night" and "*Songes.*"

For a long time *On Swedish Rhymes* was not held in high
regard, and it must be admitted that the poetic grains of gold
in the large collection are few and far between. However, calling
attention to Almqvist's observations on prosody and rhyme,
Ruben G:son Berg discusses sentiments in his verse that are in
some cases surprisingly modern.[4] Accordingly, several of the
Seseman poems have attracted increasing attention and are
now seldom absent from Almqvist anthologies.

Thus, Almqvist incorporates his last great manuscript into the
Wild Rose fiction; during his lonely years in exile, the poet again
conjures up the well-known Hunting Seat characters. With their
familiar voices, their circumstantial discussions, and lively dialogues, they must have had a therapeutic effect on their author.
The mobilization of the unforgettable setting, of his native
country, and the poetry itself must have meant a lot to the
isolated poet in his clearly wretched existence. The present site
of the Hunting Seat is specified by Almqvist in a short dialogue:

> A. But where is your Castle situated?
>   In the air . . . bless me . . . in the air, you say?
> B. The site is of no great importance
>   As long as it is a bright and happy lodging.
> A. But . . . you are anxious to get there?
> B. I have only to dream and I am there at once.
>   (*Poems in Exile,* p. 42)

III   "*Nobody knows the tone of my mind*"

Almqvist's life was eventful, varied, and comparatively long.
He was born the year after the assassination had ended Gustavian absolutism in Sweden, and he lived to see the introduction
of the bicameral parliament in 1866. When he was born, the
reign of terror of the French revolution had reached its peak;
when he died, the Civil War in the United States had just
finished.

Almqvist grew up with the Romantic phalanx and came to be the one who pursued Romantic ideas most diligently in their most diverse aspect and extreme fashion; but in his later, "realistic" period, he was the man who articulated social and political questions most eloquently, advocating new lines of reasoning and social change with merits that have not been fully appreciated unto our own time.

It is very likely that, next to Strindberg, Almqvist remains the most multifaceted genius of Swedish literature. His œuvre comprises most fictional genres, and with an enthusiasm matched by keen perception, his factual prose treats religious, political, linguistic, historical, geographic, and ethnographic subjects both in expository form and in the style of provocative journalism. He always went on writing, from his boyhood's neat sketches up to the interminable fragments of his exile and old age.

The man behind all this work, this adventurous life is, however, difficult to discern; Almqvist has been characterized as "a man of many masks."[5] The wide range of his writings corresponds to the many roles he played, both as a professional (scholar and would-be professor, farmer, teacher, clergyman, journalist, and poet) and also as an individual (mystic and rationalist, leader with standing of prophet, economic expert, devoted Christian, and heretical theologian). He is the man who analyzed Swedish poverty and European discontent, the dreamer who drew exotic arabesques, and the vigilant reformer. He is an ardent nationalist and a rabid radical, a romantic and a realist.

The contrasts and contradictions that comprised his personality—and which he himself analyzed—also confused his contemporaries, whose descriptions of the man differed considerably. During his time in Sweden he had an abundance of admirers as well as adversaries.

Almqvist's standing in Manhemsförbundet and the extant correspondence between him and its members demonstrate his rare gift for arousing enthusiasm and admiration, and for making friends. To the members of Manhemsförbundet, the memory of Almqvist as the inimitable and inspirational leader of their youth remained even after they had chosen to go their separate ways. In the 1820s and 1830s, he was the friend and correspondent of Atterbom and the Uppsala Romantics; during a later period he was held in high esteem by Thomander and the latter's friends in Lund as well as by the Liberal members of the *Aftonbladet* circle in Stockholm.

After the catastrophe of 1851, his adversaries indulged in orgies of defamation of the runaway radical and criminal. Few—with the notable exception of Runeberg—tried to distinguish between the person and his work, and not even his closest friends could keep the shocking revelations of June 1851 from coloring their earlier opinion of him.

Apart from the question of the catastrophe, other signs of hesitation and criticism were perceptible in the attitude of his friends toward their highly admired companion. He was not only a mystic but also a man of mystery. C. F. Bergstedt summed up: "Even in the most trivial matters, he would entangle himself in ingenious but pointless lies."[6] And Fridolf, the poet's devoted half-brother, said of him: "Love always had secret motives."[7] In a letter to the composer Adolf Lindblad in 1841, Fredrika Bremer spoke of "a rattle-snake look" in a comment that probably referred to Almqvist,[8] but in a later letter to the same person she said, with reference to *"Songes,"* that "Almqvist understands heaven." Emil Key, an admirer of Almqvist, thought that there was something chill, untrustworthy, and impenetrable about him. "His light, silent tread also contributed to the impression of mystery, almost of fear of the daylight, that he made in these years. At certain moments his face showed striking signs of sensuality."[9]

There is an unmistakable touch of coldness about Almqvist, who was often so warm and enthusiastic. He felt this himself and also understood its effects on those around him. Several of his letters touched on this problem; an autobiographical note has also been detected in *Amorina*, in which the heroine is not capable of showing her distress openly and is, consequently, supposed to be cold. Hierta testifies that no one could discern "any real signs of deep affection for anybody except his own family, nor did he sustain any feelings of hatred or revenge. He could be warm, even passionate for ideas but hardly for people, whom he generally seemed to look upon as chess men on life's large chessboard."[10]

It is, however, obvious that Almqvist had a quite remarkable

faculty for making contact with people of all social classes:
both friends and foes agree on that. The explanation must lie
in his genuine interest in people, combined with a normally
amiable and helpful attitude to those around him, and above
all a great charm. He knew how to move in the most varied
circles, and this amused him. In a letter to Atterbom of 1837
he wrote:

> It is odd to be sitting at dinner one day beside Countess N.N.,
> née N.N., eating pineapple, and to be dining the next day seated
> on the unpainted lid of a chest eating sour loaves and unpeeled
> potatoes, surrounded by Scanian *gräbbor* and *paukar* [dialect for
> "girls and boys"] and to be sleeping one night on bulging feather
> beds, the next night on a sack filled with straw and chaff. But one
> thrives on it; one feels so free, happy, and independent of the
> course of events. One is like a bird, at one moment picking away
> at a pile of wood-chippings, at the next moment swinging on a
> honeysuckle branch. (*Letters,* p. 118)

With these pithy lines, the poet-traveler summed up, in vivid
antitheses, the structure of Swedish society, the sources of his
own works, and his mode of artistic expression.

The contradictions in Almqvist's character accent the un-
predictable, elusive, and surprising element in his works and
his behavior. In contrast to the lucid, analytical logic of his
expositions, we see a play of the imagination, which is not only
suggestive to the reader but clearly also compelling for the
author, a game of make-believe in which truth and imagination,
art and reality at times might seem so confused as to lose their
identity. That is how both Almqvist's son Ludvig and his old
friend J. A. Hazelius saw him.[11]

But the enigmatic personality behind these contrasts in life
and literature is evasive—perhaps precisely because of its many
facets. It is a banal truth to say that each reader naturally creates
his own image of Almqvist. But it is also obvious that each
age, each generation, growing interested in particular features
of Almqvist as a poet and human, tends to see a different
persona presented in his works. His own period saw in him the
wizard of creativity, the poet of the cornucopia, and the un-
yielding opponent in religious and political questions. After

his death he was first regarded as the mysterious criminal, but from the 1890s on he was considered a Romantic and Symbolist: Ellen Key designated him as Sweden's most modern poet.[12] The mainly biographical-psychological approach taken to Almqvist in the 1910s and 1920s—and also the editing of many of his works—offered rich sources of material and incentives to the individual reader. After the 1940s it was often Almqvist, the philosopher, the mystic, and the aesthetician, who demanded attention whereas, during the most recent decades, a greater interest has been aroused by his ideas on social and political change. It is no exaggeration to say that Almqvist is our own contemporary. And yet the enigmatic poet slips away into the shadows where much remains for the scholar to illuminate. What Almqvist says in "The Song of the Moon" is still true of his own personality:

> Nobody knows
> The tone of my mind.

Notes and References

Almqvist's works have been published—though not in entirety—in a modern edition: *Samlade skrifter* (*Collected Works*) (Stockholm, 1921–38). In references this work is designated as "*CW.*" His letters are quoted, insofar as possible, from the volume, *Brev 1803–1866* (*Letters 1803–1866*) (Stockholm, 1968), shortened *Letters*. Almqvist's newspaper articles are quoted from *Aftonbladet* (*AB*), *Jönköpingsbladet* (*JB*), and *Dagligt Allehanda* (*DA*), respectively.

Chapter One

1. *Aftonbladet*, July 26, 1851.
2. Sweden proper had an area of about 175,000 square miles and a population of about 2.3 million; until 1809 Finland, with a population of about 0.8 million and an area of about 130,000 square miles, also belonged to Sweden. After the unfortunate Finnish war (1808–09) Sweden was forced to surrender Finland to Russia. However, five years later Sweden conquered Norway from Denmark as a compensation, and from 1814 to 1905 Sweden and Norway formed a union though each country retained a separate constitution.

In connection with the Finnish war, a *coup d'état* was staged, dethroning Gustav IV Adolf and replacing him with his uncle, Karl XIII. Named as successor to Karl XIII (who was childless) was J. B. Bernadotte, one of Napoleon's marshals, who reigned from 1818 to 1844 under the name of Karl XIV Johan.

In 1809 Sweden was given a new constitution, which put an end to Gustavian autocracy, and divided the power among king, cabinet, and parliament.

3. Th. Tufvesson, *Ur sekretärer och kistelädikor* (Malmö, 1918), p. 122.
4. E. Almquist, *C. J. L. Almquist. Studier öfver personligheten* (Stockholm, 1914), p. 145.
5. A. Hemming-Sjöberg, *Rättegången mot C. J. L. Almqvist* (Stockholm, 1929). English version: *A Poet's Tragedy: The Trial of C. J. L. Almqvist* (London, 1932). Hemming-Sjöberg finds Almqvist guilty whereas S. Jägerskiöld declares the poet not guilty in *Från Jaktslottet till landsflykten. Nytt ljus över Carl Jonas Love*

Almquists värld och diktning (Stockholm, 1970). Jägerskiöld's argumentation, however, has been rejected in all essentials by P.-E. Wallén in *Perspektiv på Almqvist* (Stockholm, 1973). Cf. also B. Romberg in *Samlaren* (1970) and in *Scandinavica* (1974), pp. 137 f.
6. R. G:son Berg, *C. J. L. Almquist i landsflykten 1851–1866* (Stockholm, 1928), pp. 286 f.

Chapter Two

1. H. Olsson, *Carl Jonas Love Almquist till 1836* (Stockholm, 1937), p. 42.
2. M. Lamm, "Studier i Almquists ungdomsdiktning," *Samlaren* (1915), pp. 51–198.
3. H. Olsson, *C. J. L. Almquist före Törnrosens bok* (Stockholm, 1927), p. 111.
4. Ibid., p. 128.
5. H. Olsson, *Törnrosens diktare* (Stockholm, 1966), p. 21.
6. O. Holmberg, *C. J. L. Almqvist. Från Amorina till Colombine* (Stockholm, 1922), p. 14.
7. Lamm, *Samlaren* (1915), p. 170.
8. H. Wieselgren, "Almqvist-bref från Amerika," *Samlaren* (1902), p. 117.
9. F. Schlegel, *Kritische Schriften* (München, 1964), p. 515.
10. Letter to C. J. Lénström, August 20, 1839.
11. Holmberg, *C. J. L. Almqvist*, pp. 34 ff.; Olsson, *Törnrosens diktare*, p. 26; A. Werin, *C. J. L. Almquist. Realisten och liberalen* (Stockholm, 1923), p. 214.

Chapter Three

1. Holmberg, *C. J. L. Almqvist*, p. 47 f.
2. Olsson, *Törnrosens diktare*, p. 39.
3. Holmberg, *C. J. L. Almqvist*, p. 258.
4. E. Lindström, *Walter Scott och den historiska romanen och novellen i Sverige intill 1850* (Göteborg, 1925), p. 162.

Chapter Four

1. E. M. Forster, *Aspects of the Novel* (Pelican Books, 1962), p. 75.
2. Olsson, *Törnrosens diktare*, p. 91 f.
3. *Swenska Litteratur-Föreningens Tidning*, January 29, 1834.
4. F. Bremer, *Brev*, II (Stockholm, 1916), p. 182.
5. Olsson, *Törnrosens diktare*, p. 97.

6. Ibid., p. 107.
7. A. Bergstrand, *Songes. Litteraturhistoriska studier i C. J. L. Almqvists diktsamling* (Uppsala, 1953), p. 343.
8. *Svea* (1892), p. 23.
9. F. Böök, *Den romantiska tidsåldern i svensk litteratur* (Stockholm, 1918), p. 306.
10. A. Bergstrand, p. 384.

Chapter Five

1. Olsson, *Törnrosens diktare,* p. 119.
2. I refer to Olsson's important monographic study of *The Queen's Jewel* in *Samlaren* (1919); rewritten in *Perspektiv på Almqvist* (1973).
3. Such an interpretation has been suggested by S. Almquist, *Ur C. J. L. Almquists författarliv* (Stockholm, 1920), p. 91 f., and Olsson, *Törnrosens diktare,* p. 114 f.
4. Olsson, *Samlaren* (1919), pp. 107–109.

Chapter Six

1. Cf. Holmberg, *C. J. L. Almqvist,* p. 330.
2. K. Westman Berg, *Studier i C. J. L. Almqvists kvinnouppfattning* (Uppsala, 1962), pp. 136, 150.
3. Holmberg, p. 309.
4. M. Montgomery-Silfverstolpe, *Memoarer,* vol. 4 (Stockholm, 1920), p. 196.
5. A. Werin, *C. J. L. Almqvist,* pp. 85–86.
6. Montgomery-Silfverstolpe, p. 204.
7. R. Hjärne, *Från det förflutna och det närvarande,* vol. 1 (Westerås, 1879), p. 81.

Chapter Seven

1. R. Fridholm, "Almquists marivaudage," *Samlaren* (1944); Olsson, *Törnrosens diktare,* p. 173 f.
2. K. Aspelin, "Fostran till verklighet. Några synpunkter på C. J. L. Almqvists Kapellet," in *Novellanalyser,* ed. V. Edström och P.-A. Henricson (Stockholm, 1970).
3. A. Werin, *CW,* VIII, xxiii.
4. Holmberg, *C. J. L. Almqvist,* p. 312; Fridholm; Olsson, *Törnrosens diktare,* p. 131.
5. Böök, *Den romantiska tidsåldern,* p. 313.
6. Ibid., p. 315.

186   CARL JONAS LOVE ALMQVIST

7. H. Schück och K. Warburg, *Illustrerad svensk litteraturhistoria,*
vol. 6, 3rd ed. (Stockholm, 1930), p. 329.
8. A. Werin, *CW,* IX, viii.
9. See also B. Romberg, "Den sansade kritiken och Almqvists
synpunkter på sitt konstnärskap," *Samlaren* (1967).

Chapter Eight

1. Werin, *C. J. L. Almquist,* p. 297.
2. O. Holmberg, *Lovtal över svenska romaner* (Stockholm, 1957),
p. 32.
3. Olsson, *Törnrosens diktare,* p. 163.
4. F. Böök, "Ångbåten Yngve Frey i Det går an," *Stockholms
Dagblad,* March 2, 1919.
5. K. Westman Berg, *Studier i C. J. L. Almqvists kvinnouppfattning,* p. 308 ff., and "Tendensen i Det går an," *Modersmålslärarnas
Förening. Årsskrift* (1963), p. 27 f.
6. S. Björck, *Romanens formvärld* (Stockholm, 1953), p. 26.

Chapter Nine

1. M. von Platen, Introduction to *C. J. L. Almqvist. Folkliv och
fantasi* (Stockholm, 1962), p. 9.
2. *Svea* (1892), p. 23.
3. A. Lysander, *C. J. L. Almqvist: karakters-och lefnadsteckning*
(Stockholm, 1878), p. 243 f.; F. Böök, *Essayer och kritiker 1915–
1916* (Stockholm, 1917); Olsson, *Törnrosens diktare,* p. 171.
4. Werin, *C. J. L. Almquist,* p. 311. See also G. Fredén,
"Balzac dans la littérature suédoise," in *Hommage à Balzac* (Paris,
1950).
5. *CW,* XXIV, xii.
6. A. Werin, *CW,* XXV, xvii.
7. Lindström; M. Lamm, *August Blanche som Stockholmsskildrare*
(Stockholm, 1931), p. 60 f.; B. Romberg, "Om Almqvists romankonst II" (Vetenskapssocieteten i Lund. Årsbok 1975).
8. *CW,* XXIX, vii.
9. Ibid., ix.

Chapter Ten

1. Werin, *C. J. L. Almquist,* passim; Westman Berg, *Studier i
C. J. L. Almqvists kvinnouppfattning,* pp. 330–76; R. G:son Berg,
"Vad skrev C. J. L. Almqvist i Aftonbladet?" *Aftonbladet,* August 17
and 24 and October 20, 1930; June 19 and July 3, 1932. A selection

of Almqvist's essays and newspaper articles entitled "*Det går en åska genom tidevarvet.*" *Pamfletter och polemik* has been published by F. Isaksson (1972). In G. Balgård, *Carl Jonas Love Almqvist— samhällsvisionären* (1973) some thirty newspaper articles are quoted or their contents described.

2. Among his articles on aesthetics the following may also be mentioned: "The Great Questions of Paragraph Morals and Emotional Morals" (*AB*, December 13, 1842–January 9, 1844; cf. above p. 137); the malicious but amusing "Tråkigheten, staad på uppvaktningar" ("Mr. Boredom Paying Visits," *JB*, September 29–October 20, 1846); "Några ord om romankritiken" ("A Few Words on the Criticism of Novels," *AB*, October 17, 1846); and "Om den närvarande roman- litteraturen" ("On the Prose Fiction of Today," *AB*, June 17–June 19, 1847). Among his articles on the political situation attention may be drawn to "Europas ställning i allmänhet, med särskilt avseende på Skandinavien" ("The Situation of Europe Generally, With Special Ref- erence to Scandinavia," *JB*, January 28–April 12, 1845), in which after surveying the revolutions and struggles for social reform in Europe, he hopes that the European working classes will attain "the legal status, the representative authority, and the degree of participation in social legislation already enjoyed by the Scandinavian farmer. That is *the example which Scandinavia sets Europe.*" Among the note- worthy articles on foreign policy is the series "Nordens sanna politik" ("The True Politics of the Scandinavian Countries," *JB*, February 7– February 28, 1846) which can also be said to be a commentary on and a development of the views expressed in "On the Practicability of Scandinavianism." For this work, see B. Romberg, "Om Almqvist, Schack och skandinavismen," *Svensk litteraturtidskrift* (1965). Finally among the social articles and those on domestic politics, one may single out "Folknöjen, betraktade ur en politisk ståndpunkt" ("Popular Entertainment Seen From a Political Point of View," *DA*, April 3– August 1, 1839; reprinted in *The Book of the Wild Rose*, vol. 12), "En blick på representationsfrågan" ("A Look at the Question of Representation," *AB*, March 8–April 10, 1844) or "Partiernas ställning och tidningarnas förhållande" ("The Position of the Parties and the Situation of the Newspapers," *JB*, December 23, 1845).

Chapter Eleven

1. Olsson, *Törnrosens diktare*, p. 176.
2. Westman Berg, *Studier i C. J. L. Almqvists kvinnouppfattning*, chapter 7.
3. Undated letter to Vendela Hebbe, probably in the winter of 1850.

Chapter Twelve

1. Parts of *On Swedish Rhymes* have been published by E. Gamby in C. J. L. Almqvist, *Dikter i landsflykt* (Uppsala, 1956) and by F. Isaksson in Carl Jonas Love Almqvist, *Armodets son. Dikter från landsflykten* (Stockholm, 1972). I quote from Gamby's edition *Dikter i landsflykt* (*Poems in Exile*).

2. E. Gamby in *Poems in Exile*, p. 19.

3. Quoted from M. von Platen's corrected version in C. J. L. Almqvist, *Folkliv och fantasi*, p. 216. The version in *Poems in Exile* is incomplete.

4. R. G:son Berg, "Ur Almqvists Om Svenska rim," *Språk och stil* (1905) and *C. J. L. Almquist i landsflykten 1851–1866*, p. 408 ff.

5. Olsson, *Törnrosens diktare*, p. 198.

6. *Göteborgsposten*, December 2, 1878.

7. F. Almqvist's words are quoted from Olsson, *Törnrosens diktare*, p. 189.

8. F. Bremer, *Brev*, II, 178.

9. *Minnen av och om Emil Key*, vol. 1 (Stockholm, 1915), p. 166.

10. *Aftonbladet*, July 26, 1851.

11. E. Almquist, *C. J. L. Almquist. Studier öfver personligheten*, p. 143; *Nya Dagligt Allehanda*, October 20, 1866.

12. Ellen Key, "Sveriges modernaste diktare. Carl Jonas Love Almqvist," *Ord och bild* (1894).

Selected Bibliography

PRIMARY SOURCES

The following list includes only the main works or the works referred to. For details the reader is referred to J. A. Almquist, *Almquistiana* (Uppsala, 1892), which is supplemented by the bibliographies in F. Böök's essay on Almqvist in *Svenska litteraturens historia*, II, 2nd ed. (Stockholm, 1929), and in H. Olsson's chapter on Almqvist in *Ny illustrerad svensk litteraturhistoria*, III, 2nd rev. ed. (Stockholm, 1967). Almqvist's newspaper articles are registered—though far from entirely—in *Almquistiana*, which should be supplemented by Ruben G:son Berg's "Vad skrev C. J. L. Almquist i Aftonbladet?" ["What did C. J. L. Almquist write in Aftonbladet?"] (*Aftonbladet*: August 17, August 24, October 20, 1930; June 19, July 3, 1932); reprinted as *Almquist som journalist. En bibliografisk översikt över Almquists publicistik 1842–1847 med register över publicerade artiklar och recenserad litteratur* utgiven av Erik Gamby [*Almquist the Journalist. A Bibliographical Survey of Almquist's Journalism 1842–1847 with A List of Published Articles and Reviewed Books*] (Uppsala, 1968).

Vad är kärlek? En viktig fråga till vars utredande jag föranleddes genom några reflexioner under mitt sista vistande i Stockholm [*What is Love?*], 1816. Anon. (*CW* I)

Parjumouf. Saga ifrån Nya Holland [*Parjumouf*], 1817. Anon. (*CW* I)

Handlingar till upplysning i Manhemsförbundets historia [*Informative Documents regarding the History of Manhemsförbundet*], 1820. Anon. (*CW* II)

Om Manhemsförbundets föreslagna organisation [*On the Proposed Organization of Manhemsförbundet*], 1821. Anon. (*CW* II)

Om brottsliges behandling [*On the Treatment of Criminals*], *Hermes*. Samling av avhandlingar, no. 1, 1821. (*CW* II)

Om enheten av epism och dramatism. En aning om den poetiska fugan [*On the Unity of Epic and Drama*], *Hermes*, no. 2, 1821 (*CW* II)

Guldfågel i paradis. Poesiens legend [*Goldbird in Paradise*], *Opoetisk calender för poetiskt folk*. Vinterhäftet 1821. Anon. (*CW* III)

189

190   CARL JONAS LOVE ALMQVIST

Rosaura. Sagan om behagets vingar [*Rosaura*], *Opoetisk calender*. Sommarhäftet 1822. Anon. (CW III)

Amorina. Den förryckta frökens levnadslopp och sällsynta bedrifter [*Amorina*], 1822. Anon. (CW III). [Unfinished, destroyed edition. Republished in 1839; see below.]

Svensk rättstavningslära [*Swedish Orthography*], 1829. Anon.

Linearteckning, ämnad att grundlägga och förbereda undervisningen uti matematik [*A Manual of Linear Drawing*], 1830.

Räknekonst för begynnare eller praktisk aritmetik [*Arithmetic for Beginners*], 1832. Anon.

Svensk språklära [*A Swedish Grammar*], 1832.

Fria fantasier, vilka betraktade såsom ett helt, av Herr Hugo Löwenstjerna stundom kallades Törnrosens bok, stundom En irrande hind [*Free inventions, which, looked upon as a whole, were sometimes called by Herr Hugo Löwenstjerna The Book of the Wild Rose, sometimes A Roving Hind*] [*The Book of the Wild Rose*. Duodecimo edition I–XIV, 1832–1851.]

Bd I. *Jaktslottet* [*The Hunting Seat*], 1832. Anon. (CW V)

Bd II. *Hermitaget. Vargens dotter.* [*The Hermitage. The Daughter of the Wolf*], 1833. Anon. (CW V)

Bd. III. *Hinden* [*The Hind*], 1833. Anon. (CW V)

Bd. IV. *Drottningens juvelsmycke* [*The Queen's Jewel*], 1834. Anon. (CW VI)

Bd V. *Ramido Marinesco* [*Ramido Marinesco*], 1834. Anon. (CW VII)

Bd VI. *Baron Julius K*°*. Om sättet att sluta stycken* [*Baron Julius K*°*. Dialogue on How to Finish Pieces*], 1835. Anon. (CW VII)

Bd VII. *Signora Luna. Colombine* [*Signora Luna. Colombine*], 1835. Anon. (CW VII)

Fria fantasier eller Törnrosens bok. Ny fortsättning [*Free inventions or The Book of the Wild Rose. New sequel*].

Bd VIII. *Återkomsten. Araminta May. Urnan* [*The Return. Araminta May. The Urn*], 1838. Anon. (CW VIII)

Bd IX. *Kapellet. Palatset* [*The Chapel. The Palace*], 1838. Anon. (CW VIII)

Bd X. *Godolphin. Svenska fattigdomens betydelse. Skaldens natt* [*Godolphin. The Significance of Swedish Poverty. The Poet's Night*], 1838. Anon. (CW VIII)

Bd XI. *Skällnora kvarn. Friherrinnan* [*Skällnora Mill. The Baroness*], 1838. Anon. (CW IX)

Bd. XII. *Herr Hugos akademi. Vad är penningen? Poesi och politik. Folknöjen. Storhetens tillbedjan* [*Herr Hugo's Academy. What is Money? Poetry and Politics. Popular Entertainment. Worship of Greatness*], 1839. Anon. (CW IX)

Bd. XIII. *Målaren. Prästens ställning* [*The Painter. The Clergyman's Situation*], 1840. Anon. (CW IX)

Bd XIV. *Den sansade kritiken* [*Sober Criticism*], 1851. Anon. (CW XV) (*Sober Criticism* is also included in the imperial octavo edition, part 2, 1849.)

Lärobok i geometrien [*Manual of Geometry*], 1833.

Grekisk språklära till ungdomens tjänst vid högre och lägre undervisningsverk [*A Greek Grammar*], 1837.

Praktisk lärobok i franska språket. I [*A Practical Textbook of French. I*], 1838.

De vita et scriptis Francisci Rabelæsi 1–2. Diss. acad. Lund, 1838. (CW IV)

Essai sur le caractère principal de la poésie présomptive de l'avenir, 1838. (CW IV)

Det går an. En tavla ur livet [*Sara Videbeck*], 1839. Anon. (CW XVI)

Törnrosens bok eller fria fantasier, berättade på Jaktslottet hos herr Hugo Löwenstjerna [*The Book of the Wild Rose or free inventions related at Herr Hugo Löwenstjerna's Hunting Seat*]. [*The Book of the Wild Rose*. Imperial octavo edition. 1–3, 1839–1850.]

Del. 1. *Jaktslottet* [*The Hunting Seat*, enlarged with *The Man Who Hated God*]. *Skönhetens tårar* [*The Tears of Beauty*]. *Semiramis* [*Semiramis*]. *Under hoppets träd* [*Under the Tree of Hope*]. *Ferrando Bruno* [*Ferrando Bruno*]. *Månsången* [*The Song of the Moon*]. *Vargens dotter* [*The Daughter of the Wolf*]. *Björninnan* [*The Bear*]. *Ifrån Leonard* [*From Leonard*]. *Ormus och Ariman* [*Ormus and Ariman*]. *Fader, o säg mig–* [*Father, o tell me–*]. *Isidoros av Tadmor* [*Isidoros of Tadmor*]. *Marjam* [*Marjam*]. *Nyniannes röst* [*The Voice of Nynianne*]. *Det doftar i skogen* [*The Scent of the Forest*]. *Uppvaknandet* [*Awakening*]. *De sju sångerna under tälten* [*The Seven Songs under the Tents*]. *Om hälsans evangelium* [*On the Gospel of Health*]. *Människans stöd* [*On the Support of Man*]. *Melia* [*Melia*]. *Svangrottan på Ipsara* [*The Swan Cave of Ipsara*]. *Schems-el-Nihar* [*Schems-el-Nihar*]. *Arthurs jakt* [*Arthur's Hunt*]. *De två chorerna* [*The Two Choruses*], 1839. Anon. (CW XIII)

Del 2. *Songes* [*Songes*]. *Livets hjälp* [*The Help of Life*]. *Gianera* [*Gianera*]. *Mythopoiesis* [*Mythopoiesis*]. *Minnesfest den 1 april* [*Commemoration on the First of April*]. *Sviavígamál* [*Sviavígamál*]. *Håtuna saga* [*Håtuna Saga*]. *Sigtuna saga* [*Sigtuna Saga*]. *Valtuna saga* [*Valtuna Saga*]. *Odensala saga* [*Odensala Saga*]. *Den sansade kritiken* [*Sober Criticism*], 1849. Anon. (CW XIV–XV)

Del 3. *Europeiska missnöjets grunder* [*The Causes of European Dis-*

192   CARL JONAS LOVE ALMQVIST

content]. *Varför reser du?* [*Why Do You Travel?*]. *Det går an* [*Sara Videbeck*]. *Murnis* [*Murnis*]. *Silkesharen på Hagalund* [*The Silk Hare of Hagalund*]. *Purpurgreven* [*The Purple Count*], 1850. Anon. (*CW* XVI)

Amorina, eller historien om de fyra, 1–2 [*Amorina*], 1839. Anon. (*CW* X)

Människosläktets saga, eller allmänna världshistorien förenad med geografi I. Det stora Asien eller det inre och egentliga Österlandet, i äldre och nyare tider. [*The Saga of Mankind*], 1839.

Arbetets ära [*The Nobility of Work*], 1839. (*CW* XII)

Grimstahamns nybygge [*Grimstahamn's New Settlement*], 1839. (*CW* XII)

Gustaf Wasa i Dalarne [*Gustaf Vasa in Dalarne*], 1839. (*CW* XII)

Ryska minnet i Norrköping eller ryssarnas härjning i Sverige år 1719 [*Russian Memory in Norrköping*], 1839. (*CW* XII)

Ladugårdsarrendet [*The Farm Lease*], 1840. (*CW* XII)

Amalia Hillner. Roman. 1–2. [*Amalia Hillner*], 1840. (*CW* XXIII)

Om svenska uppfostringsväsendet [*On the Swedish Educational System*], 1840.

Svensk språklära, tredje upplagan översedd och tillökad med samlingar över tio svenska landskapsdialekter [*A Swedish Grammar,* 3rd ed.], 1840.

Gabrièle Mimanso. Sista mordförsöket emot Ludvig Filip i Frankrike, hösten 1840. Roman. 1–3. [*Gabrièle Mimanso*], 1841–42. Anon. (*CW* XXIV)

Tre fruar i Småland. Roman. 1–3. [*Three Ladies in Småland*], 1842–43. Anon. (*CW* XXV)

Ordbok över svenska språket i dess närvarande skick. Del I, ht 1–2. (A-Brand) [*Dictionary of the Swedish Language*], 1842, 1844.

C. J. L. Almqvist. Monografi, samlad och utg. för att lätta översikten och bedömandet av vissa bland tidens frågor [*Monography*], 1844–45.

Smaragdbruden. Följderna av ett rikt nordiskt arv [*The Emerald Bride*], 1845. Anon. (*CW* XXVIII)

De dödas sagor. Med ett föregående brev om den skandinaviska Nordens betydelse för Europas fornhistoria [*The Tales of the Dead*], 1845. Anon.

Om Skandinavismens utförbarhet. Föredrag hållet i det skandinaviska sällskapet den 4 februari 1846 [*On the Practicability of Scandinavianism*], Köpenhamn, 1846.

Syster och bror, en av Stockholms hemligheter. Romantiserad berättelse [*Sister and Brother*], 1847. Anon. (*CW* XXIX)

Herrarne på Ekolsund. Roman från mediet av förra århundradet.
1–3. [*The Ekolsund Counts*], 1847. Anon.
Fria fantasier för piano-forte. Häft I–II. [*Improvisations for the Pianoforte*], U.å. (1847–48).
Samlade skrifter. Första fullständiga upplagan, med inledningar, varianter och anmärkningar. Under redaktion av Fredrik Böök utgiven av Olle Holmberg, Josua Mjöberg, Emil Olson och Algot Werin. Stockholm, 1921–38.
This edition, *Collected Works*, was planned to comprise 32 volumes but only 21 appeared: I–X, XII–XVII, XXIII–XXV, and XXVIII–XXIX.
Dikter i landsflykt. I urval utgivna jämte en inl. om Almqvistkatastrofen av Erik Gamby [*Poems in Exile*], 1956.
Murnis eller De dödas sagor, utg. av Erik Gamby [*Murnis or The Tales of the Dead*], 1960.
Hvad är en tourist? Brev och korrespondenser från en utrikes resa, med inledning och kommentarer utgivna av Kurt Aspelin [*What Is a Tourist?* Letters and Correspondence from a Journey Abroad], 1961.
Källans dame. Utkast och fragment med inledning och kommentarer utgivna av Kurt Aspelin [*The Lady of the Fountain. Drafts and Fragments*], 1966.
Brev 1803–1866. Ett urval med inledning och kommentarer av Bertil Romberg [*Letters 1803–1866*], 1968.
"Det går en åska genom tidevarvet." Pamfletter och polemik. Urval av Folke Isaksson [*"The Age is Hit by Thunder!"* Pamphlets and Polemics], 1972.
Armodets son. Dikter från landsflykten. I urval av Folke Isaksson [*The Son of Poverty. Poems from Exile*], 1972.

Of Almqvist's works the following have been translated into English:

Gabriele Mimanso, The Niece of Abd-el-Kader, or an Attempt to Assassinate Louis Philippe, King of France, trans. G. C. Hebbe (New York, 1846).
Sara Videbeck—The Chapel, trans. A. B. Benson (New York: ASF, 1919, 1972).

SECONDARY SOURCES

This list is a restricted selection of Almqvist criticism. The books and papers listed here I have found useful in preparing my book. They are also intended to give a general and introducing survey

194 CARL JONAS LOVE ALMQVIST

to a hundred years of Almqvist research. For a more detailed study of this research I refer to B. Romberg, "Almqvistforskning 1869–1966" (*Svensk litteraturtidskrift*, 1966).

AHNFELT, ARVID. *C. J. L. Almqvist, hans lif och verksamhet*, Stockholm, 1876. The earliest monograph on Almqvist.

ALMQUIST, ERNST. *C. J. L. Almquist. Studier öfver personligheten*, Stockholm, 1914. Psychological study. Certain specifications in reference to Almqvist's biography; some material not printed before is made accessible.

ALMQUIST, JOHAN AXEL. *Almquistiana*, Uppsala, 1892.

ASPELIN, KURT. "Carl Jonas Love Almqvist eller Det oavslutade skrivsättet." [Introduction to] C. J. L. Almqvist, *Källans dame. Utkast och fragment* med inledning och kommentarer utgivna av Kurt Aspelin, 1966.

————. "Fostran till verklighet. Några synpunkter på C. J. L. Almqvists Kapellet" (*Novellanalyser*, under redaktion av Vivi Edström och Per-Arne Henricson, Stockholm, 1970).

BALGÅRD, GUNNAR. *Carl Jonas Love Almqvist—samhällsvisionären*, Stockholm, 1973. A suggestive and engaged study of Almqvist's criticism of society. In his evaluation of certain parts of Almqvist's later writings he differs from earlier research. However, he does not always do full justice to this research.

BERG, RUBEN G:SON. *C. J. L. Almquist i landsflykten 1851–1866*, Stockholm, 1928. Describes the exile's shadow-like existence. A very valuable monograph of Almqvist's last obscure years.

————. *C. J. L. Almquist som journalist. En bibliografisk översikt över Almquists publicistik 1842–1847 med register över publicerade artiklar och recenserad litteratur*, utgiven av Erik Gamby, Uppsala, 1968. Duplic.

BERGSTRAND, ARNE. *Songes. Litteraturhistoriska studier i C. J. L. Almqvists diktsamling*, Uppsala, 1953. A detailed and suggestive study of the *Songe* poems, their origin, and music. Should be supplemented with Lennart Breitholtz' "Almqviststudier" (*Samlaren*, 1953).

BJÖRCK, STAFFAN. "C. J. L. Almqvist. Romantic Radical" (*The American Scandinavian Review*, 1969). Reprinted as introduction to C. J. L. Almqvist, *Sara Videbeck-The Chapel*. Translated from the Swedish by Adolph Burnett Benson, New York, 1972.

BREITHOLTZ, LENNART. "Almqviststudier," *Samlaren*, 1953. The main part of this study reprinted as "Songes-studier" in *Perspektiv på Almqvist*, 1973.

BÖÖK, FREDRIK. "Almquist-studier" (*Essayer och kritiker 1915–1916*, Stockholm, 1917).

————. "Carl Jonas Love Almquist," *Svenska litteraturens historia,* II, 2nd ed., Stockholm, 1929.

HAGEDORN THOMSEN, HANS. "Androgyneproblemet i Almqvists roman Drottningens juvelsmycke," *Kritik,* 1970.

HEDIN, GRETA. *Manhemsförbundet. Ett bidrag till göticismens och den yngre romantikens historia,* Göteborg, 1928. Historical ideological perspectives and biographical data of the members of the Society. The main part of the book is devoted to Almqvist.

HELLSTEN, STIG. *Kyrklig och radikal äktenskapsuppfattning i striden kring C. J. L. Almqvists "Det går an,"* Uppsala, 1951.

HEMMING-SJÖBERG, AXEL. *Rättegången mot C. J. L. Almqvist,* Stockholm, 1929. Translated into English *A Poet's Tragedy: The Trial of C. J. L. Almqvist,* London, 1932. A scrupulous jurisprudential study which finds Almqvist guilty of the crimes he was accused of.

HOLMBERG, OLLE. *C. J. L. Almqvist. Från Amorina till Colombine,* Stockholm, 1922. Almqvist's literary development in the 1820's and 1830's. Among other things important points of view of Wild Rose aesthetics.

————. "Almqvist och mordets filosofi," *Svensk litteraturtidskrift,* 1971. Reprinted as "Almqvist—mordet, självmordet och dödens trädgård" in O. Holmberg, *Kärlek, ensamhet och dödens trädgård. Tre sentimentala kapitel från svensk romantik,* Stockholm, 1972.

ISAKSSON, FOLKE. "En politisk människa," [Introduction to] *Carl Jonas Love Almqvist, "Det går en åska genom tidevarvet." Pamfletter och polemik.* Urval av Folke Isaksson, Stockholm, 1972.

JÄGERSKIÖLD, STIG. *Från Jaktslottet till landsflykten. Nytt ljus över C. J. L. Almquists värld och diktning,* Stockholm, 1970. An interesting but methodically not satisfactory attempt to free Almqvist of the charges of 1851, which gave rise to a lively debate among the scholars. Jägerskiöld's argumentation is rejected in all essentials by Per-Edwin Wallén in "Some aspects of the question of Almqvist's guilt" (*Perspektiv på Almqvist,* 1973). Cf. also B. Romberg, *Scandinavica,* 1974.

KEY, ELLEN. "Sveriges modernaste diktare. Carl Jonas Ludvig Almqvist," *Ord och bild,* 1894; in book form 1897. A devoted study rich in intelligent and striking observations. Paved the way for the Almqvist renaissance of the 1890's.

KJELLÉN, ALF. *Sociala idéer och motiv hos svenska författare,* I–II, Stockholm, 1937, 1950. Looks upon Almqvist's novels and journalism in the 1840's in relation to the social trend of the literature of that period.

196   CARL JONAS LOVE ALMQVIST

LAGERROTH, ULLA-BRITTA. "Almqvist och scenkonsten," *Perspektiv på Almqvist*, 1973.
LAMM, MARTIN. "Studier i Almquists ungdomsdiktning," *Samlaren*, 1915. Analyzes the influence of Swedenborg and Swedenborgianism on Almqvist up to his Värmland period. Fundamental to the modern study of Almqvist.
LYSANDER, ALBERT. C. J. L. *Almqvist: karakters– och lefnadsteckning*, Stockholm, 1878. A penetrating and scrupulous monograph; an important basis of all subsequent research in connection with Almqvist.
OLSSON, HENRY. "C. J. L. Almquist, Drottningens juvelsmycke. En diktmonografi och en orientering," *Samlaren*, 1919. An outstanding study rich in material and results. A central part of it was thoroughly revised and published under the title "Om komposition och huvudteman i Drottningens juvelsmycke" in *Perspektiv på Almqvist*, 1973.
––––––. C. J. L. *Almquist före Törnrosens bok*, Stockholm, 1927. A meticulously precise, comprehensive and inventive study of Almqvist's life and literary production up to the end of his Värmland period.
––––––. *Carl Jonas Love Almquist till 1836*, Stockholm, 1937. A comprehensive image of Almqvist, based on modern research.
––––––. *Törnrosens diktare. Den rike och den fattige*, Stockholm, 1966. The best introduction to Almqvist.
––––––. "C. J. L. Almqvist," *Ny illustrerad svensk litteraturhistoria*, III, 2nd rev. ed., Stockholm, 1967.
PAGROT, LENNART. "Almqvist och den romantiska ironien," *Samlaren*, 1962.
PLATEN, MAGNUS VON. "Medlidandets dikt. Carl Jonas Love Almqvist: Häxan i Konung Carls tid," *Svenska diktanalyser*, under redaktion av Magnus von Platen, Stockholm, 1965.
Perspektiv på Almqvist. Dokument och studier, samlade av Ulla-Britta Lagerroth och Bertil Romberg, Stockholm, 1973.
ROMBERG, BERTIL. "Almqvistforskning 1869–1966," *Svensk litteraturtidskrift*, 1966. A critical survey of a hundred years' research on Almqvist.
––––––. "Über C. J. L. Almqvists Romankunst," *Orbis Litterarum*, 1974.
––––––. "Om Almqvists romankonst," I–II, *Vetenskapssocieteten i Lund. Årsbok* 1973, 1975.
SIMONSSON, IVAR. "C. J. L. Almquists afhandling om 'Europeiska missnöjets grunder.' Bidrag till dess proveniens," *Samlaren*, 1919. The first profound analysis of Almqvist's criticism of society.

WALLÉN, PER-EDWIN. "Några synpunkter på frågan om Almqvists skuld." *Perspektiv på Almqvist*, 1973.
WERIN, ALGOT. *C. J. L. Almquist. Realisten och liberalen*, Stockholm, 1923. An important work which analyzes and presents Almqvist's artistic development and also his association with the social and political tendencies of the day. His material is mainly Almqvist's works 1835–1840.
—————. "Brottslingen Almqvist," *Nya Argus*, 1930; reprinted in Werin, *Den svenske Faust*, 1950, och i *Perspektiv på Almqvist*, 1973. Criticizes and supplements Hemming-Sjöberg's study.
WESTMAN BERG, KARIN. *Studier i C. J. L. Almqvists kvinnouppfattning*, Uppsala, 1962. Studies in detail Almqvist's progress and contributions as a feminist. An important chapter deals with questions of women's rights in Almqvist's journalism.
—————. "Går det an? Almqvist som könsrollsreformator." *Könsroller i litteraturen från antiken till 1960-talet*, under redaktion av Karin Westman Berg, Stockholm, 1968. Reprinted in *Perspektiv på Almqvist*, 1973.

Index